True Love *and* the Woolly Bugger

True Love *and* the Woolly Bugger

Dave Ames

THE LYONS PRESS
Guilford, Connecticut
An imprint of The Globe Pequot Press

The Lyons Press is an imprint of The Globe Pequot Press.

10 9 8 7 6 5 4 3 2 1

Printed in the United States of America

ISBN 1-59228-227-X

Library of Congress Cataloging-in-Publication Data is available on file.

I would like to dedicate this book to my fishing buddies who preferred to remain anonymous, but without whom none of these stories would have been possible.

CONTENTS

ACKNOWLEDGMENTS

THANKS TO the folks at my original publisher, Greycliff, for the opportunity to write these stories the way I thought they should be written.

I would especially like to thank my editors: Stan Bradshaw and Tom Harpole. They made a good team (even though they don't know each other) because Tom told me what I had done right in exclamation points, and Stan told me what I had done wrong in exclamation points. Their penciled notations of "WOW!!!" and "YUCK!!!" in the manuscript margins provided the proper blend of focus, discipline, and encouragement I needed to finish strong.

Dave Ames
1996

True Love *and* the Woolly Bugger

The Woolly Bugger

1964. FOR THE generation of American baby boomers staring the next millennia in the face Bob Dylan said it best with his new song: "The Times They Are A-Changin'." The distance casting competition for trout flies was won with an average of just over 156 feet. When Christmas finally came I was ten years old, on vacation with my family in Florida, and tormenting my mother as only her child can.

"All right," she cried finally in exasperation, "Go fishing. See if I care."

"Hey, thanks Mom," I said. "You're all right. I don't care what the neighbors say."

Her glare could have fried bacon through a lead shield, but quickly, before she could change her mind and sentence me to hard time at the kitchen sink, I zipped under the green canvas awning of my grandparent's trailer home to the hoosey-house to get my fishing gear.

The hoosey-house, stinking of sulfur, stained with hard-water iron, and cluttered with life's odds and ends, appeared to be merely a bathing shed, but to me, a northern farm boy, it was enchanted with an air of preadolescent mystery. The worn grey concrete block building was always dark and cool even in the subtropical heat, shrouded in climbing vines and strange orange orchids that bloomed only at night. The dank inside corners were home to various mosses and mildews, and sometimes black cockroaches so large and fearsome they haunted me even in my dreams.

I pushed open the door, and peeked inside. No bugs today. *Phew.*

I grabbed my tackle and whistled my way along the cracked shuffleboard courts, under the palms, and across the swinging bridge where the shrimp fleet gathered. I leaped onto the boardwalk fronting the pink stucco drugstore, and scooted past the rattan chairs where the locals gathered to gossip over morning Cokes and coffee.

The first old man in the row jerked a thumb at me. "That one ain't very big now, is he?"

"An' kinda young to be fishin' alone, don't you think?" replied the next old man in the row as he scratched at his leg above the white knee sock. The comments continued as I scurried down the gauntlet of wrinkled brown snowbirds who had retired to a life of tropical ease:

"Skinny too."

"Hope the wind don't blow too hard."

"Forty knots and he's a Cuban."

"Could always put a string around his ankle and use him for a kite."

I ignored them all because it was my mother's point exactly, and the public fishing pier was now only a short cast away. One deep breath and I left the land behind, for it was the smell of the pier that I loved the best. The scent was promise, as much texture as odor, a nearly palpable fusion of sunshine and hurricanes, of salt air and fish fillets, of sea breezes and brine-soaked pilings, and the exotic perfume of the pier wrapped me like skin until my small fingers could almost touch the strange lands far across the sea.

The pier, I had learned from a picture postcard, was at that time the longest fishing pier in all of Florida. I decided as I walked that also meant it was the best, then I stopped at the covered bait shack which teetered near the end of the pier. The man behind the counter was shiny with sweat. Faded blue anchors were tattooed on his forearms, and his greasy white T-shirt was stretched across the taut round belly of a professional beer drinker.

"What'll it be kid?" he said over the hum of the pumps that were constantly circulating cool seawater through the tanks of live bait behind him.

I held up my pasteboard bucket. "A dozen shrimp, please. Big ones."

"That'll be a buck even."

"It's all I have," I replied, crossing my fingers for luck and handing up the two quarters, three dimes, and two nickels which was all I had been able to glean from under grandma's cushions.

The man counted. He shook his head no, then shrugged, and grunted, "Close enough. But no more deals. I gotta make a living too."

"Thanks mister," I said, and watched happily as he dipped his net into the live well.

The crescent moon hung low in the amber of the western sky. The tide was coming, and the pier was crowded with fishermen. I pried open my battered green tackle box, and pawed through the brown lump of rusty tackle for a hook, and a weight hefty enough to bend that stiff steel pole of my youth. I baited up and let fly.

"Must be pirates offshore, eh sonny?" said the fisherman next to me.

"Huh?"

"That sinker of yours hits like a cannonball."

"Oh, no," I fretted. "Is it too heavy? Will it scare the fish?"

"Scare 'em? Hell, it might kill 'em."

As it turned out, I did have a problem, but scaring the fish wasn't it. The fish were out there, I just couldn't catch them. They stole the bait time after time, and inside of an hour I was down to my last shrimp, wondering how I was going to come into another dollar, when I finally hooked a fish—a small jack that was about a foot long.

"I have to land this fish," I thought. "Then I can use it for bait and keep fishing."

Which is exactly what happened—after a fashion.

The jack was thrashing on the surface when a passing pelican mistook the helpless fish for an easy meal. The bird in one fluid motion dropped from the sky and with long splashing beak swallowed whole my fish. The pelican then paddled away, tail-feathers wriggling in contentment, oblivious to the fact that he was well tethered to an angry ten year old with twelve-pound monofilament. Intent on teaching the thieving bird a lesson, I gave the line a good hard yank.

The pelican squawked as his head was suddenly jerked under the water, then my scrawny reel moaned as the bird flapped into the air. In its frantic effort to escape the pelican swung to-and-fro on my line like a Chinese fighting kite, crisscrossing line after line of the shoulder-to-shoulder fishermen stuffed along the pier rails. Habituated to dining on fish scraps and attracted by the commotion, more pelicans entered the fracas, until the air was so full of swooping birds and tangled lines that there was hardly room for all the bad words.

One thing about fishermen—especially old ones—they sure know how to cuss. The epithets were in at least two different languages, and ran the gamut of what can be done with and to all of the various body parts, but basically, they were simply creative variations on a common theme:

"Get that bird the chingada hell outta here amigo, or you'll need two mules and a burrito to pry it outta yer little culo!"

Although it would be several more years before I learned to speak Spanish, I already knew I didn't want a burrito anywhere near my culo. Even so—even though nobody wanted to get rid of that bird more than I did—I was helpless. I panicked, and then I panicked some more. I was frozen in place, with no more chance of moving than a bunny rabbit paralyzed by the headlights of a screaming eighteen wheeler; then, gruff and piercing above the hubbub, a single voice rose.

"I'll take care of him."

A grizzled man advanced down the dock, drawing a knife from a sheath of leather stained dark with the dried blood of dead fish. He stared with his one good eye as he approached, now so close that the grey stubble on his chin sparkled in the sun. I had been reading the comic book version of Moby Dick and, ever the victim of an overactive imagination, all I could think of was Queequog, his harpoon, and my mother.

Mom was right, I thought as Queequog clomped closer. Convinced that divine retribution for sassing back to my mother was upon me, and my blood was about to mingle with that of the poor dead fish, I pleaded with the Powers that Be for mercy.

Please, I promised, *From here on out, I'm nothing but good — really, really good.*

The Powers aren't dumb. They knew I was lying.

The Powers had heard it all before from every other kid who ever existed, and Queequog, his tattered clothes stained with a lifetime of spilled rum and fish guts, never even slowed down. The metal spike on his wooden leg ripped splinters from the plank decking, flecks of spittle glistened in the whiskers below the drooping left corner of his mouth, and his eyes slashed like cold wind. He shook his cutlass. He flashed the brutal smile of a man who has killed a thousand whales, and wasn't about to let a puny cabin boy get in his way. "This'll fix you," he growled. He raised the cutlass high above his head, and the blue steel sang as the blade arced down toward the cowering cabin boy one step before the mast.

"NO-O-O-O!" I screamed as loudly as my fear-engorged lungs allowed, which was considerable. Queequog leaped back with a scream of his own. He dropped his cutlass, and disappeared. The cabin boy blinked, and to his amazement an old fisherman materialized out of thin air, a man who was just now picking himself up off the deck of the longest fishing pier in all of Florida.

"Good Gawd boy!" he said and slapped his leg, "Y'all scared the livin' bejeezus outa me."

"I thought, well, I just thought, maybe, you might have been somebody else."

"Somebody else? Well I guess. Yer eyes was bugged out big as the noon-day sun."

"I'm sorry m-m-mister," I stammered. "I guess m-maybe it was the knife."

"Well, y'all kin rest easy now. I ain't a gonna hurt you, I jes' wanna cut yer line."

The bird flew off. The old men lining the rails chuckled at the excitement, and I found I had a batch of newfound friends who, among other things, shared shrimp and squid and stories. They taught a new dog old tricks, like how to rig a sliding sinker so the fish could not so easily abscond with my bait. Slowly, life on the pier settled back to normal, but for me, life would never again be quite the same.

I had discovered adrenaline.

1966. Bombs fell on Hanoi for the first time in the Vietnam War. Frank Sinatra won the Grammy for album of the year for the last time, and the Woodstock sixties began in earnest. Although I was still too young to fully appreciate the significance of this event, I had my own mind-expanding experience in the form of my first-ever truly great day of catching.

I was part and parcel to a multi-family vacation in northern Ontario, canoeing the lakes of Algonquin National Park. We were camped on a small lake named Provoking near a rocky point after a long morning of portages. The tents were set up, lunch eaten, the dishes clean, and everyone else was asleep in the oppressive midday heat.

Massive white thunderheads built against the blue sky above the green forest. The humid air was thick and sticky as cotton candy and swallowed whole the rustle of the leaves, the chirp of the birds, and even the breeze. "Might as well go fishing," I thought because I never could take naps (until I got to college), and I decided to go out on the rocky point where I hoped it might be cooler.

The pregnant silence of the calm before the storm was broken only by my crackling footsteps in the dry brown pine needles on the forest floor as I walked alone to the lake. I slipped and stumbled through the broken granite boulders to the tip of the point. I rinsed my head in the cool water, then cast lethargically, and began a half-hearted retrieve.

A smallmouth bass smashed the Rapala minnow as it began to dive. The fish leaped into the air, fighting desperately for his freedom, which he earned when he zigged and I zagged on his third jump. Another fish smashed the lure before I was sure the first one was even gone. One cast, two fish.

"Not bad," I thought. "Not bad at all."

I had blundered onto a pack of smallmouth bass that, due to my own dumb luck, a cold spring in the lake, or perhaps the approaching storm, were bellicose despite the sultry weather. The fish attacked the lure time and again. Nearly every cast I caught and missed bass after bass until the storm finally exploded over the lake. The fish quit biting, and I returned to the tent camp, where everyone was standing around under the rain tarp.

"You're all wet!"

"But Mom," I replied, "It's raining."

"Don't 'But Mom' me." My mother crossed her arms and tapped her foot. "You don't have any more dry clothes since you fell out of the canoe this morning. What's the matter, you never heard of a raincoat?"

I looked at the ground and mumbled, "It wasn't raining when I left."

"Next time, take your raincoat."

I looked up and nodded that yes, in the future, I would predict it.

"So, how was the fishing?" she asked.

This was a subject I had hoped to avoid, and I stalled politely for time. "Could I have some Kool-Aid please."

My mother handed me a paper cup. "You never answered my question," she repeated as she poured. The Kool-Aid was cherry red. "How was the fishing?"

I peeked at the other fisherman in the group, their open ears wide like lying eyes, awaiting my reply. There was only one rocky point on the lake. I could only hope the Powers weren't listening, because everybody else was.

"Slow," I replied, wondering at the celestial penalty for fibbing to your mother, and, oddly enough, ready to accept it. "Pretty darn slow."

1979. Ayatollah Khomeini seized American hostages in Iran. Three Mile Island nearly lit up the eastern seaboard. On a warm day in May, I met the Rainbow People.

I remember it well. I had recently moved to Montana, and stream season had just opened. It was a Friday, it was springtime in the Rockies, and I was home from work early.

I was talking with my friend Lee in the shade of the apartment building in which we lived. We were jump-starting the weekend, sprawled in the lush green grass next to a dented cooler full of ice and beer. Ostensibly, Lee and I were planning a fishing trip, but mostly we just watched the prairie slope of the foothills above the buildings, where half a dozen Rainbow girls, not a tan line among them, fairy danced through the fragrant wildflowers, stooping now and again to pluck a blossom here or a plant there.

Down below, the hot spice of tempura and Thai peanut sauce seared the breeze, sharing the airwaves with the concussion of Led Zeppelin blasting from several strategically located speakers. The Rainbow People—a name taken collectively by an eclectic assortment of humanity with a common longing for simpler times— were cooking.

In form, as they highball along the express lane to Nirvana, the Rainbow People most resemble the loosely structured American Plains Indian tribes of a century ago. Individually, they range from happy feet and tree huggers to astrologers and witch doctors, and together they form an amorphous group that gathers from the odd corners of the world each summer in a free-for-all camp-out to celebrate the karma of all that is natural.

The Rainbow gathering that year was scheduled for later in the summer in the mountains near Yellowstone Park. Roving bands of Rainbow-driven nomads and gypsies merged like streams into rivers as they closed in on Yellowstone; a large group had erected tents and tipis in our back yard in Helena that afternoon. They were visiting the Reverend Stumbo, who, for tax purposes, was the first and only disciple of The Church of the Immaculate Prospector, and who lived next door in the old yellow school bus with the three flat tires.

"How long will you be here?" I had asked of a Rainbow boy as I offered him a cold beer.

"Hey, wow, like a day or a lifetime," he said, then drained the can in one effortless swallow, finishing, "it's all the same to me."

It was, perhaps, the Rainbow credo. Montana, at that time, was an anything-goes kind of place, but even so—even given the fact I lived in an apartment complex my father had described as a damned commune full of dirty hippies wearing somebody else's clothes—those Rainbow girls on the hillside were a real eye-opener.

"Don't stare," said Lee.

"I can't help it," I replied.

Lee plucked up a blade of grass. "Makes it hard to think about fishing."

"Makes it hard to think, period," I agreed.

Having lived a relatively sheltered life, raised according to the strict edicts of fundamentalist Baptist doctrine, it was nearly impossible for me not to gawk at one amazing Rainbow girl in particular, who had rumbled in astride a chrome, chopped, hot pink Harley strapped to a rod case conspicuous by its presence.

After a perfunctory "howdy do," she had scampered through the flowers to join her friends in the celebration, along the way shedding layer after layer of nothing but black leather (including things I had no idea could even be made out of leather) and silk, revealing a collection of intertwined serpents—polychrome vipers and pythons and adders—that corkscrewed up her long leg from writhing ankle to rounded breast.

"That's a lot of tattoos," I said.

"How long would it take?" Lee grimaced. "Just think of all those needles."

"Maybe she's into pain."

"Hey, look." Lee pointed. "I think she's coming over here."

"What do you suppose she wants?"

"I told you not to stare. Now you're in trouble."

"What do we do now?" I asked. "Should we take off our clothes or something?"

"Too late," said Lee, and we fell silent as she approached.

The woman set her flowers on the ground, and stood up straight. "No pockets," she said, raising both hands palm-up, fingers-spread to prove it. "Got a spare dip?"

So that was it. No problem. Lee reached into his hip pocket for the Copenhagen.

"It's fresh. Dated the seventeenth."

"That's great. Thanks." She took the can, then whacked it against her palm to loosen the tobacco, and stuck a black-olive-sized wad in her lip. She packed it with her tongue, then spit enthusiastically. Some Rainbow People, it appeared, were more pure than others.

"Man, I gotta quit this shit," she said.

"Everybody wants to, and nobody can." Lee pulled out his own monster dip and finished:

"Nicotine's the worst."

The girl nodded emphatically and rocked back on her heels. "You got that right."

It was quiet while we reflected on the greater truths, then the girl introduced herself.

"I'm Julie," she said, folding her lean body down into the grass next to the cooler. Julie rolled onto her back, then clasped her flowers tight to the spitting cobra due north of her right breast, and nearly purred with satisfaction as she buried her head in the bouquet of living color.

Lee pointed to the flowers. "For the dinner table?"

"Nope." Julie pulled her head out of the flowers. "For diarrhea." She stroked a hanging yellow, graceful, bell-shaped, spurs-off-the-back kind of flower. "This is yellow columbine."

"Did you say diarrhea?" I asked.

"Yep." Julie flicked a lady bug from her stomach. "Montezuma's revenge. I use it in Mexico. It really works—it's a traditional native medicine. You boil the roots."

"No kiddin'? What about the others?"

"Here, smell this." Julie crushed the feathery green leaves of a small white flower, and held it to our noses on the breeze.

"That's wonderful," Lee agreed, and it was—sticky sweet and pungent.

"*Achillea lanulosa*," said Julie, "common yarrow. Named after Achilles at the battle of Troy, where it's said she used it to stop the bleeding in her troops after the fighting."

"*She?*" I thought.

"And this is fireweed." Julie wiggled a tall plant laden with lavender flowers. "We're going to boil the shoots for dinner like asparagus."

Oh. There's a reason people don't eat more weeds. "How's it taste?" I asked.

Julie changed the subject. That was a bad sign. We could only hope fireweed was better than tofu. "So, what are you guys up to?" she said.

"We were just talking about fishing Beaver Creek tomorrow morning," replied Lee.

"I see you're a fisherman," I added, striving mightily to be nonchalant, gesturing toward the rod case on her bike.

"Fisher*man*?" She stressed the last syllable, eyebrows arched. I tried again.

"I see you're a lady who likes to fish." It was all the invitation Julie needed.

"You're right," she said. "So, what time we leavin' ?"

Lee and I looked at each other. It's only the things you don't do that you regret.

"About five," replied Lee.

"Five!" Julie was clearly astonished. "Why so early? The hatch isn't until noon."

"Hatch? What hatch?"

"The stoneflies. This time of year, there's an afternoon hatch of little yellow stoneflies."

"Flies?" Lee sounded a bit disgusted. "That crap? We use worms."

"Worms!" Julie jumped to her feet. "I can't believe it."

"You can't believe what?"

"I can't believe I'm talking to a bait fisherman."

Lee was defiant. "And I can't believe your feet touch the ground when you walk."

"Bank maggot."

"Tweed sucker."

They glared at each other, and then Julie giggled.

"You a bettin' man?" she asked.

"Sure," replied Lee.

"Here's the bet," said Julie. "I can get there at noon and catch more fish in an hour than you caught all morning."

"No way you can do that," replied Lee. "What's the wager? And remember—a woman should never gamble more than she can afford to lose."

Julie considered. "Dinner and a deep body massage. And remember—a man should never gamble more than he can afford to lose."

Lee considered. "Sorry, I can't do it."

"What's the matter?" Julie flapped her arms and clucked like a chicken. "Afraid to put your money where your mouth is?"

"No, it's not that. It's just that I'm what passes around here for happily married, and I'd like to keep it that way."

"Well, then, what about you?" Julie said and looked me over then in the eye. "You got anything you can't afford to lose? If you do, tell me now, because I need to go get dressed. This evening wind is giving my snakes goose bumps."

To tell the truth, I wasn't all that crazy about a five o'clock start myself, because in those days there was little—if any—distinction between Friday night and Saturday morning. But still, a bet was a bet, and a short nap after the bars closed Lee and I crossed the continental divide, parked in a streamside meadow, and rigged rods by the dawn's early light.

"Up or down?" asked Lee. "Your choice."

"I'll go upstream," I replied.

"Well, podner, see you at high noon," he drawled in his best Hoss Cartwright, and we stumbled our separate ways under the last of the morning stars.

One mountain morning later we rendezvoused back at the road-side meadow. It was time for the showdown. Julie was already there, bent double at the waist with her palms flat on the ground, stretching in the hot sun.

"Look, it's Yoga Bear," I said quietly to Lee, but not quietly enough because Julie overheard me.

"Is that you Boo-boo?" Julie's reply came upside down from behind her long dangling brown-to-the-ground hair. She straightened as we approached, and I held out my trout.

"Five," I said, "all browns."

"You killed those fish?" Julie blinked her dark eyes in disbelief. "Boy, you got a lot to learn."

She slipped into a pair of hip boots, and slid her rod together. It was the first time I had ever seen a fly rod up close. It was long and impossibly slender, dark green, and so soft that the tip shivered like a cold nose.

"Nice pole," I said.

She laughed. "For what this cost you get a rod, not a pole—but thanks."

"I'll save my thanks for dinner. I'm going to win. It's too bright." I waved my arm to take in the hot barrage of photons beating the living daylights out of everything in sight. As far as catching fish went, I figured, we might as well have been on Mars. "They quit biting over an hour ago."

"Nope. They're just getting hungry. What it is, is you just have to be really, really sneaky."

Julie pulled on dark sunglasses and then was gone—a chameleon, brown skin, khaki shorts, and drab olive halter blending into the spring of riparian green—a mule deer, bobbing and weaving through the brush, quiet as the wind, crouching low and dropping to one knee on a gravel bar, stripping then flicking line into the choppy water at the head of a smooth run.

I have to admit, it was beautiful to watch, the stalk and cast a graceful dance above the willows, but it was clear to me that Julie was wasting her Pocohontas routine. Any old fool could see that.

I'm not just any old fool. I quickly called out, and doubled the bet (the wine to go with dinner) just in time to watch dumbfounded as the placid run was broken by a splashy rise. Julie raised her rod, and, several heartbeats later, slid a trout back into the water.

"That's one." Julie took two and three (a brown nearly long enough to tickle her elbow as she pulled out the hook) from the head of that same pool, and then stood up.

"How'd you do that?" I was incredulous.

Julie giggled. "They're hungry today, aren't they?"

"I'll say." The question was what they were hungry for. Obviously, it wasn't worms. I pointed to the end of her line. "What is that thing anyway?"

"Here, I'll show you." Julie handed me the fly.

I held it in my palm. "They eat this!" It was inconceivable.

"All the time."

I examined the fly more closely. "What is all this stuff?"

"Mostly feathers and fur."

I wouldn't have believed it, but I had seen it with my own eyes. "O.K." I said. "I concede. You win. There's just one thing."

"What's that?"

"Please," I begged. "You gotta show me how you do that."

She did, and I did, and then we did, and before I knew it, I had just forged the linchpin in a meandering chain of lifelong passion. It is a sticky chain now spread through my being like the blue steel web of a Star Trek spider, watery shackles over the years grown so long and strong that both my body and my soul are hopelessly bound to the edges where I fish with a fly.

1991. New Year's Eve. It is a subdued party among old friends. Everyone is harried from the hustle of holiday bustle and, like well-worn shoes, a bit frayed at the loose ends of the tired stitching in their souls.

"Geez, I'm beat," I said. "My kids were up at six this morning."

The Professor leaned over and speared a meatball with a toothpick, then looked at the sauce he had just spilled on his shirt and said, "This time of year is hard, isn't it?"

"It's just too busy." The Duke added a bit of eggnog to his rum. "A day isn't long enough even without Christmas thrown in."

There was a nod of collective agreement, tempered with head shakes of wonder at how quickly today and tomorrow become a year ago yesterday.

"Things sure have changed," I said. "Remember when we first met?"

"It's amazing that any of us lived," said Airbrush. "What year was that?"

"1980," replied the Professor who has a good head for numbers. "The same year Mount Saint Helen's erupted."

We reminisced around the combination cocktail/buffet table, telling story after story as we all remembered together, until with much arm waving it was as if there again we were: standing around in my kitchen, just after the fall equinox when the brown trout spawn, and just before the first big storm swept the burnished leaves from the glowing cottonwoods . . .

"Hurry up. We gotta go." The Mayor looked impatiently at his watch. "You have five minutes to get ready."

"Where are we going?" I asked, only because I wondered how long I might be gone.

"Fishing," was the simple reply.

I looked around my kitchen. I had just been invited at the last minute to join in the Second Annual Hunter S. Thompson Memorial Fishing Derby. I knew most of the men present only by their reputations as Serious fishermen; this would be an open-ended trip through the blue-ribbon trout rivers of Montana that seemed as if it might take a while.

"Make it six minutes," I said. "I think I better call in sick before we leave."

"There's just one thing." The Duke—the patriarch of this fishing event, and the best fisherman I have ever known—stepped forward in a T-shirt bearing a caricature of Richard Nixon with an overdrawn nose.

"What's that? I asked.

"You need a bribe."

"A bribe?" I looked around the room. "What kind of bribe?"

There was silence. You were either on the bus, or off the bus— and it was leaving. I thought frantically. "I can row," I said. I didn't know much, but I knew Serious fishermen liked nothing better than a good all-day row job. There was discussion.

"Interesting," said Airbrush, who was part owner of the local fly shop, and a full-time flyfishing guide who wanted nothing more than to get out from behind the oars for a while.

"No way," said the Duke. His superhuman capacity for sustained euphoria was legendary: if you couldn't swallow a bribe, he didn't want it.

"And a case of Wild Turkey," I said, seeing how the conversation was going and figuring this was one trip I didn't want to miss.

There was more discussion and animated arm waving. This group of equals among equals formed an amoeba of pure fishing democracy. Each individual was a pseudopod of the whole, together wondering at the mix of my ectoplasm with the single-celled bacchanalian life form into which they merged at the city limits. Finally, there was general agreement and I was absorbed.

"O.K.," said Airbrush, who helped pay the winter bills by customizing vans and drift boats on the side, and achieved immortality when he once decorated a patriotic stripper as an American flag before she jumped out of a cake at a Legion party. "You're in."

"And don't forget you're rowing," said the Professor, who holds doctorate degrees in two different sciences, but has only a fifty/fifty chance of getting his shoes on the right feet in the morning.

"Let's go," said the Mayor (of Bentonia—a small town in the mountains of southwestern Montana).

"No. Not yet." The Duke, in cocoa-brown Seal-dri latex waders that were everywhere speckled with black vulcanized tire patches, spoke up once again. "First the benediction. Who has the archives?"

"I do." A stout man named Harry stepped forward. He was dressed as a park ranger, and a daffodil yellow harmonica shaped like a banana dangled around his neck from a shiny orange strand of hay-baling twine. He played some Jumpin' Jack Flash, faded into twelve bar Chicago blues, did a little dance, then read reverently from a well-thumbed copy of *Fear and Loathing in Las Vegas*. "Now remember," he added, closing the book and replacing it in the archives, "if It's all right with you and the Universe, It's all right."

To say that I was amazed by this display of hedonism would be putting it mildly.

Nihilism, or the belief that existence is senseless, is as good a description as any of steady work, and this bunch of renegades were nihilists only to the point that they couldn't go fishing with flies. Behind every avid fisherman stands good friends—fishing buddies—and I had just met mine.

"Wow," I thought, "These are my kind of guys."

These were the people with whom, over the years, our shared passion for fishing the rivers, lakes, and oceans of the world would become in memory, until the end of old age, like pictographs in stone. Our trips together will become the rocking chair memories that will endure where others fade—the memories that will have the nurses at the Lazy Acres Home for Retired Fishing Guides wondering at the toothless grins as they come to adjust the wool lap blankets, and wipe away the drool.

"Fish 'til you puke," said the Duke now that it was time to go, and a bottle of Wild Turkey made the rounds.

I found that the cork in the bottle could be made to gobble like a tiny turkey if, when pulled, it was twisted just so. The next thing I knew I was behind the oars of a drift boat, fighting the wind on the Yellowstone River, and Harry Mason, in the front seat of the boat, was steaming.

"I thought you said you could row."

"I can row." I defended myself as best I could considering the fact that, at the time, Harry was pushing the boat from the willows with his middle leg. "I've done a lot of white water."

"That don't mean shit." Harry was quite succinct for a lawyer. "Let me give you a little rule of thumb," he added. "When you're rowing, and you're close enough to shore to spit onto dry ground — you're too close."

The problem was that I was used to running the rowdy western white water rivers, where rowing is as much scouting as it is floating, first climbing above the rapids to mark the scattered rocks and recirculating holes, then, at water level, finding and following the marks you have drawn in your mind to the slick green tongue, the churning water ear drumming your roaring skull, louder by the moment, rowing for position, hoping only to pinball down the path of least resistance, pulling so hard that at times the oars will snap like toothpicks, no matter, the oars useless anyway in the bubbles as you are buried alive in a raging flood bright as quicksilver.

Rowing properly for fly fishermen, on the other hand, is more Baryshnikov than Schwarzenegger, with (optimally) never a hard, sharp, or quick pull; but rather, here a dip, there a dip, everywhere a continuous stream of gradual nudges calculated to maintain a constant distance and angle of the boat with respect to the shore, all the while adjusting boat speed with respect to the current speed so as to maximize the fishable drift of the flies — despite the complicating vectors of fickle winds, ever-changing currents, and vast coolers filled with iced beer.

It was also fast. So very fast.

Streamer fishing as the shore went past was utter boat-wide concentration on the unfolding riverbank as deep green holes followed pockets of foam, and swirling eddies became frothing current lines: one after another, and another, and another. All the while, I saw good fishermen for the first time rocketing streamers into the pocket water like Nolan Ryan strikes: plop—strip, strip, strip; plop—strip, strip, strip; plop—strip, strip, strip, until the line tightened in the water and somebody grunted again as they set the hook:

"Got one."

"Look at that sucker jump!"

"Come on now. Double up. Double up!"

Up until this point, I was mainly a self-taught flyfisherman of the tiny mountain creeks and beaver ponds. As the odyssey of great trout rivers—the Gallatin and the Madison, the Firehole and the Yellowstone, the Big Hole and the Jefferson—continued, it was with my mouth shut and my eyes open that I began my true education as a fly fisherman.

I began to learn to row. I learned how important it was to cast to the bank ("If that streamer lands six inches away from the bank," the Duke told me, "that's six inches too far.) I saw trout caught, lots of trout, mostly on a new-to-me fly called the woolly bugger. It was a soft dark fly of turkey down, chicken feathers, and fuzzy chenille skins. It was also double wrapped with .035 lead fuse wire, tied heavy as a roll of quarters, and made my early casts such an impossible task that, whenever I stood to fish, whoever had the dangerous task of rowing took to wearing a green hockey helmet signed by Bobby Hull.

Despite the all too frequent whack of speeding lead on cursing plastic, the heavy flies hooked so many trout that I began to understand where in the river it was that the fish lived, and where it was that they were likely to feed. I saw the double and single haul, how critical to the whole of the cast was a part called the mend, and the difference between a cast that caught fish and one that did not.

"There's not much, is there?" I said.

"What do you mean?" asked the Professor, as he climbed from his sleeping bag later that week.

"I've been looking all over for some food." I said. "Don't you guys ever eat?" It was the morning of Day Four, and we still had not eaten a decent meal.

"Eat? What do you mean?" There was general puzzlement as everyone gathered around the coffee pot. Nourishment appeared to be a foreign concept. I have since read that amoebas don't eat— they assimilate.

"You know—food," I said. "Whole grain. Meat. Fruits and vegetables. Stuff like that."

"Too many rivers," said the Professor.

"There's no time to eat," added Harry Mason.

"Besides, we have food," said the Mayor as he ate the olive in his Bloody Mary.

"All four major food groups," finished the Duke.

"No way." I didn't know it, but the boys were setting me up. I took the bait by adding, "There's no food. I've looked everywhere."

"Sure we have food—" and then everybody got in their two cents worth as they warmed their hands around the campfire of cottonwood logs:

"There's Beer,"

"And Chips,"

"Coffee,"

"and Donuts,"

" —All four major food groups."

"Five if you count whiskey,"

"Just look in the cooler,"

"Or under the seat,"

"No. Don't bother—Nobody'd eat what's under the seat,"

"No matter how hungry they were."

"But don't worry—"

"The Last Supper will soon be here."

I found out later what they really meant was the First Supper.

It was Day Seven, and I wondered if I still had a job. Aside from peanuts we still hadn't really eaten, but now we were barbecuing, high at 7000 feet, and well below freezing in the Norris Geyser Basin of Yellowstone Park. Orion rose in the night sky to the south. We scarfed pink chicken, baked black beans, and charcoaled cinders of rib-eye steak. There was a shooting star. Dessert was a cake gone stale, baked in the shape of a giant breast (a 99 D?) slathered with vanilla icing, and topped with a jumbo pineapple ring and half a peach by somebody's girlfriend, or maybe (who knows?) somebody else's girlfriend to be.

Anyway, she had said, this cake is special. She wasn't kidding.

"What's this?" I asked. There was something wadded up in my piece of cake. It was a piece of cloth. I smoothed out the fabric, and held it up.

"It's a pair of rainbow panties!" I said.

"Look there's more," said the Mayor, and there were. The cake was well laced with just the right delicate guarantees to make civilization look good again. The Professor scratched his bushy beard, then held a scarlet wisp of gauze up to the noisy light of the white gasoline lantern, and inspected the label.

"Fruit flavored!" The Professor spoke with surprise. "Says here they're edible."

Harry stared happily at his pair of panties. "It ain't heaven," he said as he licked off the frosting, "but it's right next to it."

"You really supposed to eat 'em?" said the Professor, staring in disbelief as Harry started in on the next course.

Harry swallowed, coughed, then spit out a chunk of elastic waistband and said: "Underwear du jour."

Duke pounded Harry on the back until the coughing fit subsided. "How is it?" he asked.

"Mango," replied Harry and took another bite. "I think we're talking mango here."

"I ain't eatin' those," said the Professor. "That's sick. Just think where that underwear might have been."

"I am," said Harry, with the glazed-over look of someone who is a thousand miles away.

"Anything would be better than that burnt-up steak." The Duke
was matter-of-fact as he cut a pair of panties into bite-size pieces
with a knife and fork, and said, "Where's the ketchup?"

"Those were the days, weren't they?" I said as we flashed back
to the future . . .

We were back at the buffet table, and it was time to quit telling stories and go home. The party was winding down. The
balloons were loose, and another New Year had already begun.
Couples re-coupled, and talk turned to resolutions as we gathered
coats and warmed up cars, buying time before venturing into the
fresh-from-Alaska arctic air mass now lurking just outside the door.

"I'm going to quit smoking." said the Duke. "I have to. My doctor
says to just keep looking at those people that haul the green oxygen tanks on the little wheels around with them wherever they go."

"I want to lose ten pounds." The Professor stared down sadly
at what all those years of research behind a desk had done to his
once svelte figure. "Maybe twenty."

"Maybe thirty," said the Professor's blonde wife who taught
aerobics two days a week.

"I'm sending in quarterly payments to the I.R.S. this year," said
the Mayor, who now had his eyes on higher office, and was worried about appearances. "Really—I mean it this time."

"I'm going to learn Spanish," said Harry Mason. Now that his
law practice was flourishing, he was thinking about fly fishing the
world. "Maybe do a little traveling."

I listened with one ear open. From a tiny sliver off the top of
my head I could already summon up a dozen good and bad habits
I desperately needed to either lose or acquire, but, perhaps a bit
wiser after years of trying, I was weary of burdening myself with
resolutions I knew I had only a trout's chance in hell of keeping.
When it was time, I figured, I would know it—even if it was too late.

Until that time came, I would just have to do the best I could
with what I had to work with. I needed a resolution I could keep.
This year, I vowed, will be different.

It had to be something I wanted to do. It had to matter. It had to hurt, but it had to help. I would have to quit cold turkey. I knew I could do it. It was the only way.

No More Woolly Buggers, I resolved. This year I fish dry flies enough to get better at it.

1994. About thirty-five million Americans now fish with flies on what is left of our wild trout rivers. The Dead, a testament to longevity, are still Grateful. I was fishing with Harry and the Mayor, on a blustery spring day on the Missouri River. There was more sun than rain, but tiny Baetis mayflies—blue wing olives—hatched sporadically during the squalls blowing down now and again from the snow-covered mountains.

"That sun sure feels good," said the Mayor.

"Kind of silly to be fishing dry now. There aren't any bugs on the water," said Harry, who was taking his turn behind the oars.

"Silly?" scoffed the Mayor. "Hell, it makes as much sense as peein' into a head wind."

Harry and the Mayor were talking about me, and they were right. It was too bright. There wasn't a rising fish in sight. But being right wasn't enough. They wanted to rub it in too. That's what friends are for.

I was fishing from the front of the boat, and my #18 parachute Adams again drifted untouched along a foam line. I got one chance, and then my dry fly was floating in the wake of the Mayor's woolly bugger as it plopped into the foam. Yet another brown trout belly flashed golden yellow on the take.

"Put her on plane," said Harry as the Mayor got the head of the fish up.

"Skid and release," replied the Mayor as he winched in the fish. People from Bentonia don't mess around. The Mayor has given up on tippet in favor of tow rope, and can land and throw back a trout in the time it takes most people to get a proper set of the hook.

"It's good for the fish. They're back in the water before they know what hit 'em."

"Be good for you too," added the Mayor for my benefit. "You ready for a real fly? Better hurry. They're up to five bucks apiece now."

I looked at my rod. I wondered where it had all gone wrong. It was too big a question. I wasn't even sure that it was wrong. All I knew was where it had all begun.

When Julie took her rods and left for wherever it is rainbows go when the colors fade, I went on my own parade, chasing shadows and mountain trout through the soothing alpenglow. I bought a fly pole, then a fly rod, and then another and another and another until finally (like true love) I found a rod I couldn't have — because the rod had me.

The rod was sensitive as ticklish skin, deep green like the thrill of spring grass, light as fairy wings, and the first real dry fly rod I had ever owned. It was a revelation. I had only to find the fish, then the rod would quickly sing out four beats almost by itself as the fly settled just so into the crease above some sipping trout. It was magic and more fun than I had ever imagined.

Somehow, someway, at some time, I had arrived at the point where the sipping trout part no longer mattered. I would rather play the music in the rod than catch the fish. If I couldn't catch them on dry flies, I didn't want to catch them, and I couldn't stand modern rap music. It made me wonder. Is this what getting old is like?

2020. Cloning techniques are perfected, and the Beatles stage a reunion concert. Technological advances include rubidium beryllium positronic fly rods, and the newest fly lines, assembled in the zero gravity environment of the space station, are coated with a special polymer from the fourth dimension that reduces the coefficient of friction to near zero. The distance casting competition for trout flies is won with a cast of just under two kilometers.

Fly fishing is now the most popular sport in the world, and I win a trip to an English chalk stream by entering a contest on the back of a box of breakfast cereal. While I am there, I catch a legendary brown trout that has been, heretofore, uncatchable. I regale in the telling of the tale to the Halfordian purist Brits who are pissed in the streamside pub.

"I floated fly after fly over that fish, duns, nymphs, and pupa, spinners, emergers and cripples. I tried everything, first 5, then 6, 7, 8, and finally 9× tippet, from #16 parachutes to #20 compar-aduns to #24 pinpricks of gossamer. Nothing.

"But now, the fish had me going. I had to catch him. It had gotten personal.

"There was only one way. There couldn't be any splash. I had to sneak closer — it was a good thing I had just had my hips, knees, ankles, and elbows replaced. I crawled on my belly until I was directly upstream of the fish, then cast down with a sixteen-foot leader. The fly and the leader settled on the bank, and then the fly rolled off the bunch grass into the water. The fish finned, but he didn't spook.

"So far, so good. I counted four, then lifted the rod tip. The fly rose in front of the trout's nose as the line tightened. He couldn't resist the eyes. Twenty minutes later I released him."

"Eyes? On a fly?" A tall gent in boss tweed spoke up.

"Yep," I said proudly. "I like to glue doll eyes onto woolly buggers. I think it stimulates the predatory instincts of the larger fish." The tall guy gasped. He was clearly horrified.

"But, but — Can't you bloody read," he stammered, pointing at the sign over the bar. "This club is for fly fishing only."

A Light Green Rain

F OR A good while I worked seasonally, only eight months a year, as a hydrologist for the Forest Service. The winter vacations generally evolved into shoestring road trips for as long as I could afford to fish, and in one of those years, it was already the seventeenth of March.

Only a few weeks remained until my job would blossom along with the first of the purple pasque flowers on the south facing slope above my cabin back home in Montana. Until then, I remained a lagging economic indicator surfing the crest of seasonal employment that is so much a part of the western rite of spring.

It was a time in my life when I was old enough to know better, and young enough not to care. I fished for winter steelhead of the Pacific Northwest by day, and caroused away the nights—playing cowboy songs in the country bars, passing the hat for gas and breakfast money, and seeking the odd job now and again when my old truck needed a new part.

Most jobs were just too odd, and financial considerations demanded I forego the replacement of any parts not essential to making the truck stop quickly, and go at least slowly. Among other well-worn parts this included the black gasket surrounding the front windshield.

Time and ultraviolet radiation had eaten away at the black rubber until it was cracked and brittle; and now, on a winding mountain road, in a howling storm on the Washington coast, where an inch or more of rain can fall in an hour, the gasket over the windshield leaked. Badly. Right down the steering wheel and into my lap, where the wet denim of my jeans chafed at my nether regions like steel wool wrapped in an ice cube.

Earlier in the day, I had stopped at a hardware store in a small ocean-side town. The streets were empty but for a few sea gulls easing through the grey drizzle. A permanently pressed clerk stood behind the cash register inside the store.

"Do you have anything to fix a leaking windshield?" I asked.

"You bet," he nodded. "Right over here." We walked through women's nylons past electrical to paint, where he picked up a tube of silicone caulk and examined the label.

"This should do it," he said. "Says here it's guaranteed for fifty years, and it works even under the water."

"Sounds like the right stuff," I replied, "I'll take it."

It was me who was taken.

The caulk couldn't have stopped a dew in the desert, and later that night, as I drove through the storm, the window still leaked. And worse, the truck cab now reeked of toxic solvents from the curing caulk. My nose, and my eyes, burned. I was dizzy, nodding off, jerking awake, fighting off sleep, swirling around in the churning maelstrom of effervescent fumes while visions of steelhead danced in my head.

At least, I thought, *this rain should bring in some fish.*

I dreamed a river cascading from the mountains to the sea, now rising with the rain. Steelhead were skittish in the brackish tidal flats at the mouth of the channel, darting up and dropping back as the long-remembered taste of their childhood strengthened in the quickening flow. The urge to spawn was overwhelming after four years of abstinence, and then the steelhead were chasing the smell of their past upstream to an uncertain future in the dark green water.

A heavy hook-jawed male led the fish up the river. The steelhead hugged the bottom, resting only occasionally — behind large rocks in the roaring rapids, and in the rising tail-outs of the deepest runs. Chrome bright and full bodied, these were wild fish, crazed by the thought of group sex in the spawning gravels. A bright orange and yellow minnow swam by, too close, and the lead male, enraged, lashed out at the bait fish.

I felt the pull, and tightened the line. The sharp hook of the Skykomish Sunrise stuck in the corner of the steelhead's mouth. Two great shakes of his head, and then the fish rocketed out of the water in a silver spray. He leaped directly at me, and his eyes shone like headlights.

They were headlights! I jumped awake. I yanked the wheel. I caught a glimpse of a green truck as I slashed across the road and dropped into a cavernous pothole. The impact snapped the front axle, and I careened off the pavement, rolling, radiator over tail pipe toward the forest at the bottom of the road berm. The screech of ripping sheet metal stuffed my ears. A tree came through the windshield.

Now it's really going to leak, I thought, tasting for a moment the bitter bark of Douglas fir before time slipped away; until, sometime later, a voice cut through the pain that was my head.

"You're pretty lucky for a white man."

The body that belonged to the voice was a dark silhouette in a chartreuse haze. I licked my lips. I tried to talk, but the wet sticky salt of fresh blood trapped my tongue in the sounds of silence.

"This will help."

The voice died away, and fingers appeared in the fog. A hand grabbed me by the hair, and yanked my head over backwards until my mouth opened wide up into the darkness. Cool drops of soothing rain fell on my upturned face. An amber bottle appeared in the glowing mist between my eyes, and then my mouth exploded in whisky fragments.

I had been around moonshine before—while going to school, and playing music in the Appalachian hills of Kentucky and West Virginia—but this batch was, without a doubt, the strongest ever to singe my lips. I coughed and wheezed, then gasped, "That stuff could kill a guy."

"Might be the best thing the way you drive."

I sighed. He had a point. I flexed. If searing jolts of pain were any indication, everything was still attached and working. It could have been worse, and maybe it was. I still hadn't opened my eyes.

"I fell asleep at the wheel," I said. "What happened?"

"The other truck never stopped. I pulled you out of the front seat just in time."

I took a deep breath, and sat up to see just how bad it was. The air burned with the acrid orange stench of fried paint and smoking black plastic. I stared through the fog at the last guttering flames still clinging to the dead iron skeleton that was all that was left of my truck. I put my head in my hands. So far, this hadn't been a great day.

"The truck wasn't much," I said, "but my guitar was in there, and all my fishing gear."

"At least you still have your guitar. It was on the seat beside you."

"Thanks," I said. "Guitar's worth more than the truck anyway."

I turned to thank my benefactor for having saved my life as well as my guitar, but the words caught in my throat as I looked up. The man was huge.

He stood a solid six and a half feet tall, brawny in the chest, lean in the limbs, with dark skin and long black hair that hung straight like shadows down his neck. His dark piercing eyes were set above high cheekbones, and he was, far and away, the biggest Indian I had ever seen.

I kept my eyes glued to his eyes as I tilted up the bottle and poured down two big swallows, but then I started coughing so badly I barely kept the whisky down. The man's chuckle was more of a rumble, then he whacked me on the back, and said to call him Red. Red then took back the bottle, and finished up by telling me to go easy on the Forty Rod because it was strong stuff.

I knew wranglers who called their whisky White Mule because it packed a kick, and good old southern boys who called their whisky Old Yeller because it made them scream, but Forty Rod was a new one to me.

"Why Forty Rod?" I asked when I had my breath back.

"Two drinks, and that's as far as your feet will take you."

I thought it over. This could be important. "How far is your truck?" I asked.

"Don't have one. I like to walk." Red grinned, then turned around. Across his back, slung from a rawhide shoulder strap, was a battered, leather, kidney-shaped case that could mean only one thing.

"You're a fiddler!" I said in surprise because you don't meet many, especially that big. "What are you doing way out here? All alone. In this rain?"

Red tapped his fiddle case. "You're not going to believe this," he said, "but I was looking for a guitar player. My last one didn't show up, the party is about to start, and the banjo player is waiting for us. Come on: It's not far."

Red picked up my guitar and started up the hill into the woods. I wobbled after him. I didn't see that I had much choice. It was a little strange, I figured, but then, that was why I was in the Olympic Peninsula in the first place.

The Peninsula is more than a place, it is a way of life, in some ways little changed since 1889, when John Muir said that "in these Washington wilds, living alone, all sorts of men may perchance be found — poets, philosophers, and even full blown transcendentalists." Nowhere was it blown more fully than in "Home" — a small colony of anarchists living north of Tacoma near the turn of the century, where the flower children of nineteen-sixties Haight-Ashbury would have fit right in.

The Home colony founders sweetened the politics of anarchy with a vigorous jigger of free love. Men and women came from far and wide to share in the noble experiment. The local newspaper, The Demonstrator, explored these issues in depth.

The Demonstrator dealt with issues such as whether women have the same rights as men in sexual relations, and whether it was possible for two women to live happily with one man. Monogamy was called the worst of all forms of prostitution, the church was described as the mother of all whores, and the paper was banned by the postal service as being obscene.

Far from being obscene, the paper was too mild for the tastes of some of the residents of Home. One woman published a pair of pamphlets entitled "How to Free the Earth of the Sex Disease" and "Clothed with the Sun." These manuscripts were rejected by the editors of The Demonstrator as "not in good taste," which, all things considered, makes one wonder just exactly what anatomical detail entered into her lessons on the nature of passion, pleasure, and the God-given rights of women.

And wonder I did as we walked down the trail. Just thinking about it exactly started me to whistling a little tune. God, it was good to be alive! I caught up to Red.

"So, where's this party?" I asked.

Red looked back over his shoulder. "At a place called Molly O'Brien's. Molly runs a roadhouse just north of here."

"Great," I said, because the night was young, I still ached all over from the wreck, and beer is more fun than aspirin. "What kind of place is it?"

Red's chuckle rumbled again. "It's a logger's bar. Molly always said that once her boys get to drinking, it's the kind of place a rattlesnake wouldn't take its mother."

"Sounds like a logger's bar all right," I agreed, then we walked into a clearing, and just like that, we were there. Whatever else Molly was, I could see right off that she was not a slave to the principles of preventive maintenance.

One of the L's in her name was missing from the sign on the roof. Yellow shafts of light poured through the vertical cracks between the rough-sawn fir boards that served as siding. The whole building leaned toward the equator like wild prairie rye in a north wind, swaybacked as a camel, buttressed from collapse to the south by a massive stone chimney.

A shed roof spanned the front of the building. Generations

of hearts and loggers' initials had been carved into the porch posts, so much love and so many names over the years that the whittled graffiti had transformed the columns into a cellulose swiss cheese of intertwined alphabet orgies. The settin' benches against the wall were shiny from years of comfortable dungaree polish, with log rounds strewn about just right for slouchers to use as footstools. The plank decking by the front door was chewed from the corks of loggers boots, and the freshly splintered wood was yellow with sap. Bright sparks from the huge chimney burst into the sky, and the heaviest of the soaring embers fell back to the roof, hissing as they winked out in the wet green moss cushioning the weathered grey cedar shingles.

We walked up onto the porch. "It's a wonder this place hasn't burned down," I said. "I'll bet it's dry as tinder underneath that moss."

"Maybe it'll go up tonight. That is, if you can get that fiddle going hot enough."

It was a woman's voice, deep and throaty, and the words came through the front door from the bright light inside the saloon. I squinted, but it was like looking into a flashbulb after our walk through the dark woods. I couldn't see a thing, but the voice had me looking forward to the time when I could.

"Molly," said Red.

He walked with open arms through the front door. I followed Red into the golden light. My eyes slowly adjusted to the glow, and the first thing I saw was a large green shamrock hung like Christmas mistletoe above the entrance. I had forgotten. It was Saint Patrick's Day.

It was Patrick before he was martyred who finally drove the snakes from Ireland, and in honor of the occasion, the good saint himself had stopped by Molly's for one or two. He stood in the corner, hand hewn from a bolt of cedar, thrusting a snake impaled on a trident clenched in his right fist toward the ceiling. In his other hand he cradled a glass of carved beer.

It was an Irish bar all right. I turned around. A stout woman with nice corners and zesty green eyes had Red engulfed in a bear hug. "It's been too long," she said to Red as they held on to their hug at arms length, smiling as only best friends can do. "Where do the years go?" Then she looked at me. "And who's this?"

"Molly," said Red, "Meet the new guitar player."

"What happened to the old one?" I asked, looking around the bar. The mayhem was considerable. It looked like a fight or several could break out at any moment.

Molly elbowed me. "We ate 'im," she said and laughed deep from the belly, then stepped aside as a wizened man stomped in from the rain. "Well, if it ain't ol' Tom Murphy," she cried.

Old Tom shook off his hat and hit it on his leg. "Hey Molly," he said, "How's the whisky this year?"

"Don't you worry none." Molly grinned. "We strained out the snakes just this afternoon."

"Why'd you go to all that trouble?"

"We have to keep the fiddler happy."

He looked at Red. "Musta worked," said Tom as he disappeared into the throng that spilled out to all four walls.

"Musta worked is right." Molly steered us toward the bar. "These boys is already knockin' around like a bunch o' blind dogs in a butcher shop," she said, "and the music ain't even started yet."

The long bar was a solid plank of oiled hemlock, notched along the edge with dozens of small half-moons. Names, written in black India ink, had been scrawled by each notch. The wall above the counter was covered with polished mirrors. Above the mirrors was a picture of the Greek goddess Venus, lounging on velvet cushions, clad in gossamer, attended by an army of long-tongued imps. Somebody had given her a green mustache in honor of the holiday.

"Saturday night art," said Molly, pointing at the picture.

Nothing new there—the back walls of the oldest taverns all across the West sport similar decorations, a throwback to frontier days when every saloon had its own patron painted lady on the back wall. It was the crescent shaped notches in the front of the bar I really wondered about.

"Molly," I said, rubbing the edge of the counter, "These missing chunks look like they have teeth marks."

Molly nodded. "Its teeth all right. Once they get drunk as boiled owls, it's how these lonely loggers prove to themselves who's the toughest hombre in camp."

"Or the dumbest," I replied.

"You best be watching that mouth of yours don't get you in trouble."

The advice came from behind, murmured in my ear. The deep voice was husky with whisky. Oh shit, I thought. Now I've done it. The last thing I wanted to do was get in a fight.

I had played with country bands in some tough places—mining bars during a copper strike, cowboy bars during a three-day rodeo, payday for the gandy dancers on the high line—but I had never before seen a saloon anything like this. I turned around.

"Katy," said Molly, "if that dress was cut any lower you could step through it."

"Thanks, Ma."

It had been Katy who had spoken in my ear. The biggest thing she was wearing was a banjo. Katy turned sideways to silhouette nature's bounty, and looked back across her shoulder for my approval. "Nice, ain't it?"

It certainly was. I attempted a friendly nod. Katy smiled, and moved in closer until her high, round breasts just brushed my arm.

"What's the matter, ain't you even gonna tell a girl hello?" she asked, then eased a hand behind my neck, and reached up to stroke the bump on my temple with a touch light as windblown hair. "What happened here?"

I couldn't believe how good I felt. There was no way I could talk.

Red helped me out. "He hit his head on a tree."

"You poor thing." Katy slid her fingertips slowly down my cheek, then she was all business as she turned toward the bar. Katy grabbed a pair of unmarked bottles and said, "I have just the thing for a headache."

She dumped twin dollops into a stein, then squeezed in a lemon, stirred in a spoonful of honey, and topped it all off with beer. "Rye whiskey and camphor." Katy handed me the glass. "Drink 'er down."

She put a hand on her banjo and winked. "You want to feel good if you're gonna play with me tonight."

I eyed the vile concoction dubiously. Aspirin was beginning to look pretty good when a fight broke out down the bar. Katy spun and grabbed the wooden bat hanging by the cash register. She waded into the center of the melee, took dead aim on the tallest of the heads in the knot of loggers who were pummeling each other by the poker table, and swung from the wrists. The man crumpled to the floor.

That got everyone's undivided attention right now, and the fight was over before it had properly begun. Katy bent low and gave the unconscious man a kiss on the cheek. "When he wakes up," she said, "You boys tell him the first one was free. Now take a blanket and haul him on out to the porch." She looked out over the crowd. "The rest of you behave now, you hear!"

Katy would get no argument from me. I drained my medicine as she approached, then said if she didn't mind I would just have plain beer the next time. Katy poured us both one, then stared at me over the top of her glass.

"We don't see many strangers," she said. "What're you doin' way out here in the middle of nowhere?"

"Mostly just fishing. I've been all over nowhere for the last couple months," I replied, trying my best not to stare at Katy's mostly exposed alabaster bosom by taking a good look around the room.

Everybody in the building was wearing at least a little kelly green, and some people were nothing but green—they had even dyed their hair and faces. Their clothes were old and worn, but clean: the men were dressed mainly as miniature Paul Bunyan clones; the women were done up flapper style for the party, the shiny fabric of their emerald dresses clinging to curving flesh and plunging into necklines trimmed with soft fur.

"Is it always like this?" I asked, waving my arm to take in the crowd.

Katy rolled her eyes and nodded. "Every St. Paddy's Day it is."

"Where do all these people come from?"

"It takes all kinds to live in the woods," Katy answered.

"Let's see now, that guy over there —," she continued, pointing into the corner where some strong silent types were spraying the hot wood stove with streams of tobacco juice between monosyllables, "— the tall skinny one. Now there's a fisherman for you.

"He left here one night so drunk he had to open his shirt collar to piss, but he was bound and determined to get a salmon for breakfast, so he set out to find himself a fishin' pole. He found a nice one in the third house he went through."

"But by now he's feeling awful tired, and worried about falling asleep with the pole and maybe being accused of thieving, when all he was really doing was borrowing. So he went into the woods behind the house, and put the fishin' pole in a hollow log where he could find it the next day. He was feeling pretty proud of himself the way he'd figured everything out, hiding the evidence and all, and he drifted off to sleep."

"Well, he woke up the next day in his own bed, and found out he'd stolen his own fishin' pole. Worse, he hid that pole so good, he couldn't find it. He decided about the only way he'd get that pole back would be to get drunk again, and maybe he'd remember where he hid it."

Katy stopped her story long enough to pull a cigarette from a silver case.

"Did that guy ever find his fishing rod?" I asked.

"Nope," Katy grinned, "But he's still lookin', most every night."

Katy struck a wooden match on the bar as Red and Molly walked up. Katy blew a smoke ring, then said that Red was really the guy to talk to about fishing. "Ain't that right, Red?" she finished, "Did you tell him about that pool out at your grandfather's place on the river?"

"Is that so?" I said, looking up at Red, and trying to keep the excitement from my voice. If anybody would know the secret spots, it would be Red.

Red grunted a native word I didn't understand, then described a small river, and a pool below a waterfall not far from the sea. Good fishing, he said, on sacred ground. I told Red that even though I wasn't sure how far back it had been I was pretty sure I had some Cherokee blood in me. Red said he thought it more likely I had Coyote blood in me, and in any event I should get my mind off fishing because it was time to go play music.

Katy and I pushed along behind Red to the fireplace on the far side of the room. The red and green river rocks in the chimney had been mortared up into a series of radiating spiral arms, alternating bands of ochre and olive, each arm outlined with glittering black mussel shells, and dusted with bits of polished beach glass. The pieces of glass, sparkling in the firelight, against the spirals of river rock, had the effect of twinkling stars in the dark swirl of a galaxy in the making. Six-foot logs burned in the immense firebox.

We tuned up, and I heard Red's fiddle for the first time. The tone was deep, rich, and gorgeous, and still plenty loud enough for dancing. The fiddle was so old that the patina of the spruce top was the golden hue of morning light shining through a thick piece of amber.

I tapped Red on the shoulder. "Where did you get that beautiful fiddle?" I asked.

It was then that I discovered Red wasn't a full-blooded Indian.

Red told me that his great-grandfather, Seamus Connery, the tallest man ever to work the Cornish tin mines, one day up and left with nothing but this fiddle (and here Red held the instrument up), and a desire to see the world. Seamus survived a shipwreck in the Juan de Fuca straights by lashing himself to the storm-torn mainmast as it floated past. He washed up on shore the following morning with his fiddle safely wrapped in a tight bundle of oilcloth.

Seamus stood on the beach playing the fiddle because it helped him think, wondering what to do next, when a canoe from one of the local whaling tribes happened by. It was the music that saved him. The Indians liked the music enough that they decided not to eat Seamus even though there was so much of him; instead they paddled him to their village where in a classic fairy-tale romance Seamus eventually taught the chief's daughter how the Irish do the jig.

Red finished his story with a wink, then followed Katy as she climbed on to the makeshift wooden stage with her banjo. It was showtime, and the burly loggers began to pound the floor with their hobnailed boots.

I couldn't blame them. Katy wore a banjo like the dance of the seven veils. I climbed up on the stage. A pair of besotted loggers were down low in the front, trying to look up her dress. "Doesn't that bother you?" I asked.

"Well, it ain't the quickest way to a woman's heart, I'll tell you that." Katy shrugged, and for the tiniest of instants I saw the wind in her eyes. "But what the hell. A girl only looks good once in life, she might as well make the best of it." She looked at Red. "You got a hot one somewhere in that box of yours?"

Red cradled his fiddle along his left forearm, rather than tucked beneath his chin. He played in the traditional style of the old-time traveling fiddlers who needed to free up their mouths on Saturday nights, so they could call square dances and bow the fiddle at the same time. "Let's try 'Bull at the Wagon'." he said. "Key of A."

I knew the tune. That is part of the beauty of old time music— the songs haven't changed much in a hundred years, and most songs are fairly simple, so no matter where you go you can always play along at least part of the time.

"Bull at the Wagon" is a traditional fiddle tune that was written to capture the spirit of the bullwhackers—the men who moved civilization westward in ox-drawn wagons reputedly by the sheer force of their profanity. It is a fast, powerful tune, and in the third part, the fiddle imitates the crack of the whip and the bellow of an angry bull. It is an open invitation for anyone so inclined to bellow along, and before long you would have thought from all the whistles and braying cattle calls that we were covered with dust, ridin' drag, herding on down that Old Chisholm Trail.

The entire building creaked and groaned under the thud of heavy logging boots on the dance floor. When the song ended,

Katy waited until the bar had quieted a bit, then raised both arms. She bent forward from the waist. "Was that just the building?" Her young whiskey voice rolled out. "Or did the earth move for you boys too?"

The loggers roared back.

Katy answered with her banjo.

She played clawhammer style—plucking the melody with thumb and forefinger, while simultaneously brushing out the galloping rhythm with the backs of the other three fingers of the right hand. The crowd immediately picked up the beat. Katy looked out over the sea of clapping hands.

"You boys ready for a love song?" Katy's husky voice filled the room. "You ready for somethin' with a little rhythm?"

The loggers roared again, and Katy nodded at Red and I to come in. I followed Katy through a straightforward three-chord progression, and by the end of the first time through we had it all together with feeling. Red switched from melody to high harmony on the fiddle when the verse came around again, and Katy began to sing:

> Don't you do it by the garden gate,
> 'cause love is blind, but the neighbors ain't.
> You told that pretty girl she'd be your wife,
> Now she wants you, with a carvin' knife.

Katy had the stage presence of a string of firecrackers. She flirted shamelessly with everything she had that wiggled, bounced, or jiggled, all the while belting out lyrics sticky with ribald innuendo, and before the second song was half over Katy had that unruly band of hooligans and ruffians eating from the palm of her lily-white hand.

As the song ended Katy raised a finger suggestively to her lips. The crowd grew quiet. It was like she had single-handedly snuffed out a prison riot. "Now this next tune is based on a true story," she said, "It's called the 'Last of Callahan'."

"It seems Callahan was an Irishman (a cheap shot—at the word Irishman the crowd roared yet again) who found himself on some hard times, and he got caught at it. The vigilantes took him down to the hangin' tree, and asked him if he had any last words before they slipped the noose down over his neck.

"Well, old Callahan says 'Nope, but before you give me my last necktie, I sure would like one last chance at a little fiddlin'. It seemed a reasonable request, and a man was sent to fetch back a fiddle.

"They stood in the sun until the fiddle arrived. Callahan played a tune, and then handed back the fiddle. They spanked the horse and all that was left of Callahan is this tune, as passed along by the hangman, who didn't have anything against Callahan—just his taste in horses."

Katy looked over at Red. "Now how does that tune go?"

And on it went through jigs and reels, hornpipes and ballads, hoedowns and two-steps, until sometime later I found that we had just played the last waltz. The bar quickly emptied amid a general chorus of farewells as the crowd returned to their forest homes. Red walked over to me.

"It's time to go," he said.

I looked at Katy. She smiled. I put my arm around her. "No way," I said to Red. "I'm not leaving."

Katy put her head on my shoulder. "I'm sorry," she said, "But you do have to go."

"But why?" I said. The music we had shared that night came from a place as elemental as gravity, a place from so far within that sometimes it seemed as if we shared a single body. It isn't often that the music takes you so far. "Don't you feel it too?" I asked.

"You know I do." Katy sighed, and pushed me lightly away. "Just get here a little earlier next year." She went behind the counter and began wiping down the bar with a wet towel. "I promise you, it will be worth the wait."

"Next year?" I couldn't believe it. "Next year?" This couldn't be happening.

"Well, then, that's settled," said Molly as she buried Red in one last hug.

And then, in the time it takes for a cloud to cover a star, Red and I were outside in the damp night air and hurrying down a trail. I just didn't get it. I was lost in thought, wallowing in a sea of churning testosterone, when Red tapped me on the shoulder.

I realized belatedly he had just spoken. "I'm sorry," I said, "I didn't hear you."

"Stay close." Red was emphatic. "If you get lost out here, I won't be able to find you."

I looked up from the ground where my eyes had taken me.

The sun was already up. We were deep in the forest, following an elk trail, pushing through green fog so thick it dripped like rain from the wall of life that surrounded us. Huge tree trunks soared up, up, and out of sight in the fog. Moss, vines, and creepers coated our world with a verdant mattress of jumbled chlorophyll, a world so wet and shamrock green it was as if the weak daylight at ground level had been run through a Vegematic.

I followed close behind Red as we pushed through the dense tangle of salal and devil's club and chest-high ferns. We skirted the trunks of fallen cedar trees that formed impassable twenty-foot-high walls in the jungle. Sometimes we even crawled through the springy peat loam, going low to slip beneath the worst of the undergrowth. It was so wet that we might as well have been under-water, and I wondered if this was how a mayfly nymph in a moss-choked river must feel.

"Careful!" Red said.

I ducked too late. A thorny branch of salmonberry snapped back and raked me across the face. I wiped the blood from my cheek with the back of my hand.

"Where the hell are we?" I asked.

"I thought you wanted to go fishing," said Red.

I had forgotten. His grandfather's place.

"This place where we're going," said Red, "It's special to my people. The story is told in the winter lodges that it was here in this river, in the pool below the waterfall, where the first of the salmon brothers appeared among my people."

And then Red's voice changed, as if he were reciting something the way he had learned it. To imagine the voice, imagine the soothing rhythm of rain falling on a tent with you warm and dry inside, and every now and again a high wind for excitement.

"Long ago, when mountains could still speak, there were no fish in the rivers. Our fathers and mothers had almost nothing to eat, and their flat bellies growled. The winter was long. When the people were nearly dead, a young boy was sent to ask north wind for help.

"North wind heard the boy, and blew out over the ocean. He talked to all the animal people. After a time the chief of the salmon people agreed to help. He came from his lodge deep in the sea to visit the boy in his dreams. The chief told the boy what to do.

"The boy scrubbed himself with sand by the river, until his skin was rough and pink like the flesh of a salmon. He took up a heavy rock, and dove headfirst in the water. The river spit the rock and boy back to shore, and the boy lay coughing on the beach.

" 'I am not yet clean enough to meet the salmon chief,' he said to himself. 'I must be pure, for the salmon people will give their lives so that my people may live.'

"For four days, he fasted, and rubbed his skin with sand; and each afternoon, as before, the river spit him back up on the land. On the fifth day, he scrubbed until his skin was nearly gone from his body, and you could see some of his bones. The boy made a great dive into the water.

"There was no splash. Now, he was ready to see the chief of the salmon, and the rock sailed with the boy along the bottom of the river to the deepest ocean. A door opened in the mud in the bottom of the sea.

"Behind the door was a lodge. Many fires burned to keep out the chill of the cold ocean, and the salmon people walked about. Their skins were drying on willow racks hanging from the ceiling. Without their skins they looked just like we do. There were so many salmon people in the lodge that it was hard to move.

" 'We welcome you as a brother,' said the chief of the salmon people.

" 'It is a great honor,' said the boy. The salmon chief and the boy squatted by the brightest fire, where it was warmest.

" 'Your vision is strong,' said the chief, 'and you can bring the salmon people to your lands, to feed your people, but first, there is a thing you must do.'

" 'My people are starving,' said the boy. 'What would you have me do?'

" 'Now, the lodges of the salmon people are crowded. Now, we cannot fill the rivers as Tyee intended, for whale is too strong. He eats us as we leave the fires. You must help the salmon people bring back the bones of whale, so we can make certain magic and have power over whale to swim freely in all the seas.'

"The boy nodded, but he wondered how he would do this thing, for whale is strongest of all the fish, and the boy knew that he was but one, not yet fully grown, and yet weak with hunger.

"The salmon people put on their skins. From extra skin they made another suit for the boy, and they swam from the lodge together a school of warrior salmon. They traveled only a small way when a great black and white whale came like a sharp arrow from the deep water and began to eat the salmon people.

"Then the boy knew what to do, for he had many friends. He called out to Thunderbird for help. The giant bird came from his nest in a cave in the cliffs high on Mt. Olympus, and swooped down on the whale. Thunderbird was so big and black that his shadow blocked out the sun, and the ocean grew dark.

"North wind saw Thunderbird helping the boy and the salmon people. North wind became jealous, and filled the ocean with a great storm of thunder and waves and lightning. Thunderbird did not care. Thunderbird sang strongest of all.

"Thunderbird's curved talons sliced into the blubber of the whale. The wings of Thunderbird pounded and the wind and waves grew even larger as Thunderbird struggled to lift the huge whale from the sea, and so it is, even to this day, that the great storms tell us when Thunderbird flies to feast on whales.

"Thunderbird carried the whale off to his cave to eat. He spit the skull on the beach, and the boy picked up some bone for the salmon chief, then swam back to the door in the bottom of the sea. The chief took the bones, and showed the boy certain magic.

" 'Watch with care,' said the chief, 'what must be done.'

"He showed the boy the way in which the bones from the first salmon caught each year must be returned to the sea, so that the spirits of the salmon people could find their way back to their lodges, and make new skins, to return each year, one after another. He showed the boy how to care for the flesh, and how the people should never take more salmon than they could eat.

" 'In this way,' the chief said, 'salmon people will fill the lodges on both sides of the ocean until the seas will rise and fall no more forever.'

" 'It shall be done,' said the boy. He put on his salmon skin and swam back to his people. The boy showed everyone the salmon magic, and ever since, in the time of the first blossoms, our brothers have filled the rivers."

Red's deep voice, the measured cadence of his sentences, and the dense fog had brought me to the brink of another time and another place. I could nearly smell the salt air and wood smoke as I stood in a village full of longhouses, watching a flood of salmon in the pristine water of a rushing river. I shook my head to clear it.

"Those runs must have been something," I said. "I've read journal accounts of the old trappers describing rivers so full of fish you could walk from one shore to the other without getting your feet wet."

We broke through the underbrush onto a small rocky cliff above the river. On hands and knees we peeked through the brush, over the cliff rim, into a pool below a waterfall. The river was small by coastal standards, high but fishable, and surprisingly clear following the non-stop rain of the previous day and night. The pool was black with fish, more steelhead than I had seen in the rest of the winter combined. If I couldn't have walked on their backs, I could have at least hopped.

Red took his knife and cut a long slender sapling. He trimmed the branches and tied on a length of stout line. In a day full of surprises, I was in for one more. Red was going to fish with a stick. We were going native.

"I'm surprised you don't just use a stone spear," I said, thinking next year a fly rod would be an appropriate token of my appreciation for the generosity he had shown me.

"No, just a bone hook." Red handed me the fly at the end of his line.

The carved hook was wrapped with fur, and long blue feathers were tied in spey style, the blue so deep it was nearly black, but iridescent like peacock herl, and the fly seemed to glitter with a faint light all its own as I held it up to the green shadows under the forest canopy so high above.

"What kind of feathers are those?" I asked.

"Great blue heron. It's my secret pattern."

I rubbed the fly. "In this light," I said, thinking about how flies attract fish, "it's almost like these feathers are glowing." I looked up at Red. "Show me how it's done."

"Wait here." He vanished into the brush, and reappeared just upstream on a gravel bar. He coiled line, then swept the long branch in a wide circle above his head, flipping the stick toward the far bank when the circle was complete.

As the rod tip goes, so goes the line, even when the rod is a stick. The line circled like a giant hula hoop, and then turned on end to unravel across the river, straightening just above the water. The bone hook plopped down next to the far bank.

Red immediately began throwing a series of upstream mends into the line, teasing the fly laterally across the river. A white mouth winked open and shut. The tail-walk was bright above the dark water, then Red threw a loop in the line to release the fish in the middle of the river.

"The jump is the best part for me," he said, and handed me the stick. "Your turn."

I grabbed the stick, and wiggled it in front of me to test the flex as I would with a new fly rod. Not bad. It had worked surprisingly well for Red. "What kind of wood is this?" I asked.

"Yew," he said.

That made sense, since it was yew from the Sherwood Forest that stocked Robin Hood's armory, and good bow wood should be good rod wood. I visualized Red's hand and body movements during his effortless cast, then I made my first cast ever with a two-handed rod. Red was right. It was a secret fly.

The secret was getting it in the water. I never did get the hang of loading the long rod, and spent as much time in the trees as the river, but I still hooked so many fish I lost count. It was like bluegill fishing when the fishing is good—except the fish were bright as quicksilver, fresh from the sea, and as big and strong as fifty or sixty bluegills put together.

We fished below the falls until the light began to fade. Red said it was time to go, and reached up beside the waterfall, into a dark crevice in the cliff of ancient black lava, and pulled out a glass jar. The whisky never looked better.

"To the day," said Red.

I grinned, and nodded. "Phew," was all I could say.

We toasted, and Red put the glass jar back up in the crack in the cliff. We found a good elk trail, and in no time at all Red was leaving me at the road, which is where I woke up the next morning with a hangover that would go at least five stars.

I was covered with frost, black-and-blue with bruises, and sleeping in a field next to the burned-out hulk of my old truck, using my guitar case as a pillow. I sat up, squeezed my temples with the heels of my hands, and swore not for the last time never to drink whisky again.

I hunted up some cardboard from the roadside, and dug out the black felt-tip pen I keep stashed inside my guitar case for just such emergencies. Montana Or Bust, I scrawled with trembling hands. Hitchhiking is always easier with a sign; two trucks and a traveling salesman later I was home.

It was a busy year, mostly because I tried to remodel my cabin, and I had no idea what I was doing. The house (and the tools I had to buy to fix what I had destroyed) ate so much time and money that I missed my winter vacation, and it was not until the fifteenth of March the following year that I was able to get out of town.

"Two days will be plenty of time to get there early," I thought.

You see, I hadn't forgotten about Katy or her promise of a year ago. I would have had to have my blood pumped to forget about that. I'd even reminded Katy about her promise once or twice with a dozen long-stemmed roses.

One thing I had forgotten about was the old truck factor. The transmission in my new truck (which wasn't really new at all — just different) dropped onto the pavement at the top of Lookout Pass on the Montana-Idaho border in the middle of a spring blizzard. I got a tow job through the snow into a Wallace chop shop.

The mechanic rubbed his chin. "Couldn't do 'er fer less than, say," and he added numbers in a greasy notebook, "Say, five hunnerd. Yer tranny's plumb shot."

"Five hundred!" I said, then asked, "How long will it take to fix?"

"Be at least a couple a days." The mechanic looked sad, but I had the feeling he was grinning inside all that grease. "Parts gotta come all the way from Seattle."

"That's too long." I was adamant. "I have to be somewhere tomorrow."

"Next day air," he said, "maybe, but it's expensive, and I'll have to charge you a percentage."

"Do it," I said, because I had no choice and he took credit cards; then the mechanic ordered the wrong parts so I got to pay for it twice and I was still late. I drove all night long but I didn't get to Molly's bend in the road until after sunrise on the eighteenth of March.

That's odd, I thought. There were a couple of houses in the trees, and a small cafe surrounded by spring flowers glowing red and yellow in round planters, but there was no bar. I turned off the truck, and sat in the front seat.

Better go ask someone in the cafe, I thought. It has to be around here someplace.

The matronly waitress behind the gleaming white formica counter looked up when I walked in through the screen door. "You all right?" she said, "You're lookin' kind of pasty in the face."

"I think I could use a little food," I said. "I've been driving all night. What's the special?"

"Just the best damn biscuits and gravy you'll find in this lifetime."

"Sounds good."

"Good! My biscuits got good beat all to hell. Coffee?"

"Only if it's as good as the biscuits."

"Ain't nothing that good," she finished. "Now go wash up. Looks like you could use it."

I lathered away the long night on the road in the bathroom sink, drying my face with the tail of my shirt, because the towel dispenser had been ripped from the wall. In its place was a blunt message scrawled in black magic marker: "Wood and paper products no longer available—Wipe your ass with a spotted owl."

It is not the fault of the spotted owl that there is a shortage of saw logs, any more than it is the fault of the logger that the forests are nearly gone. The owl and the logger are both losers in the race to sell our forests, a race being won by a few people with Swiss bank accounts. I didn't say anything because in that country, to be vocally sympathetic to the plight of the owl is to invite a severe thumping. Besides, I had other things on my mind.

"Any bars around here?" I asked, back at the counter, cradling hot coffee in cold hands.

The woman looked out the window. "Little early to be drinkin', ain't it?"

"Most days," I agreed.

The cook's bell rung, and the woman went to get my breakfast.

"Italian sausage and real cream, now that's the trick to gravy," she said when she returned. "Pound of sausage for every pint of cream." She looked me over, and folded her arms across her chest. "Used to be a bar here, but it burned down."

I spoke between mouthfulls. "I just thought I'd stopped at a bar around here is all."

"Not likely." The woman shook her head. "The last bar here burned down in 1927."

"How can you be so sure about the year?" I asked. "That was a long time ago."

"I even know the date," she said. "March 17 — St. Patrick's Day. I know because half the people in town was burned up in that fire during a big party. Includin' my grandma. It ain't an easy thing to forget."

"You ever hear the name of that bar?" I asked.

"Well, hell, everybody round here heard of Molly. She run the most famous sportin' house in the history of logging right across the road there." The woman's eyes opened wide. "Say you ain't the weirdo that keeps sendin' flowers are you?"

"Not me." I smiled uneasily, and added, "These biscuits sure are flaky."

"You want flaky biscuits, you gotta keep the butter in the freezer." She eyed me suspiciously. Suddenly, I wasn't hungry anymore. The room was too small. I needed fresh air.

"Too many miles and too much coffee," I said, and paid the bill. "I just need to go for a little walk."

I cut across the highway, back into the trees, and there, in a tangle of briars and berries, stood a massive old chimney, laid up in dark spirals of river rock, inlaid with bits of glass that glittered in the sun like twinkling stars. It was, without a doubt, the same chimney that had buttressed Molly's ramshackle building from collapse.

It didn't take me long to figure out what had happened. There was a simple explanation.

A year before, I had been thrown from my truck when it rolled down the hill. Knocked unconscious and suffering from a concussion, I slept while my mind drifted away without me. I had seen the chimney on another trip, and incorporated the beautiful rock work into my dreamworld. The same with the river. The rest was wishful thinking and coincidence, the by-product of an overactive imagination.

I just needed to go fishing. The river would clear my head.

Although I now walked logging roads through clear cuts, I found the river I remembered. This time there were no fish stacked like cordwood in the pool, and the crack in the cliff of dark basalt beside the frothing white waterfall was empty. Still, I broke into my pack, and pulled out my gifts—the pack rod and the new reel, the strings for fiddle and banjo, the aged Kentucky bourbon, the little black dress—and hid it all (not all the bourbon) deep within the crack in the cliff.

Another year passed, and once again I found myself at the waterfall, but this time I spooked a pair of steelhead from the pool as I came in too quickly. I stopped and counted ten, breathing deeply, willing myself to slow down. Then I checked the crack.

The gifts were gone; in their place was an old Mason jar.

The lid was rusted away, and the jar was full of dead bugs and twisted cobwebs. The jar also held some long blue feathers that had been neatly tied to a carved bone hook. The iridescent fly glowed with a faint light all its own as I knotted it to my tippet, and I settled back to wait under the trees in a light green rain beside the singing river.

An Invitation

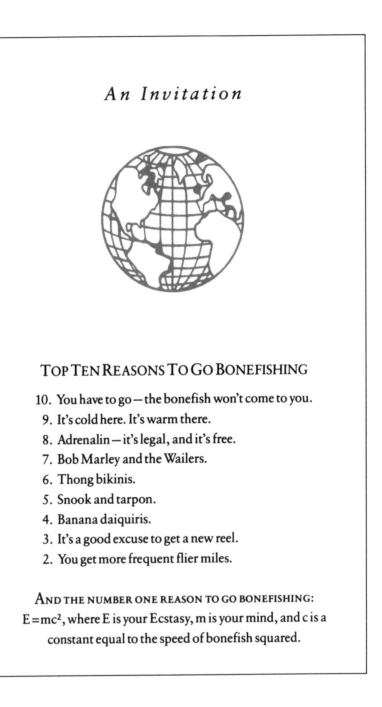

Top Ten Reasons To Go Bonefishing

10. You have to go — the bonefish won't come to you.
9. It's cold here. It's warm there.
8. Adrenalin — it's legal, and it's free.
7. Bob Marley and the Wailers.
6. Thong bikinis.
5. Snook and tarpon.
4. Banana daiquiris.
3. It's a good excuse to get a new reel.
2. You get more frequent flier miles.

AND THE NUMBER ONE REASON TO GO BONEFISHING:
$E = mc^2$, where E is your Ecstasy, m is your mind, and c is a
constant equal to the speed of bonefish squared.

Ju-Ju Travel

BONEFISHING

I SCANNED through the trip details in the following pages of the invitation. Round-trip airfare (including inter-island shuttles) for under five hundred dollars. We would be camping on a beach, under the palm trees, next to a bar and restaurant. There were bonefish flats within walking distance. It sounded too good to be true.

"If there was a Hall of Fame for travel agents," I thought, "The Duke should be enshrined."

As usual, I was broke. Although the trip would be cheap, it wouldn't be free. I had never before been bonefishing, but had always wanted to try it. I would just have to sell something.

I won't miss the truck. I'm still not sure about my soul.

That's Ju-Ju.

It all began with the highest winds yet, gusting to thirty knots. Duke and I were hunkered back to the wind on a weathered cypress dock, deep in the heart of the Caribbean, watching the sun rise, sucking coffee, waiting for our guide.

"There he is." Duke pointed to Garfield's red boat smashing through the whitecaps.

I watched the boat wallow through the wave troughs up to the dock. "I'd hate to see you get seasick on your birthday," I said.

The Duke threw his fishing bag down into the boat. "Fish till you puke," he replied.

"Goddom it!" Garfield called up from his boat. He spoke Carib, a staccato and melodic blend of several different languages, including English and Reggae. "Diss win' fury lok all bad hell mon."

"It sure is," said Duke.

"Heymon?" Garfield spit sentences like bursts of machine gun fire on full automatic. "Dat cas' might be dere no way dis day?"

"It will be all right," said Duke.

"Goddom mebbee?"

"No worries mon," replied the Duke.

I stared blankly at the two of them. It sounded familiar, like something I should be able to put together, but all I picked out was a whizzing bullet of a word here or there. It was so very, very fast. I turned to look at Duke. "What's going on?" I asked.

The wind caught the brim of my hat as I lifted my head, and it sailed off the dock. Duke jumped into the boat, then plucked my hat from the swells. "Garfield wants to know if we can cast in this wind," he translated.

I set the wet ball cap firmly back on my head. "We'll have to try. It's too early to go sit in the bar."

"Crazymon." Garfield laughed with delight as we roared off to sea. "Dem fly whack de head dis day, I see dat."

We were fishing a submerged volcano in the lee side of the Lesser Antilles. Unlike the other towering islands in this archipelago, we fished a land low and flat, a classic coral atoll crowning the peak of a sunken mountain, pulverized by hurricanes through the millennia into an ellipse of white sand and powdered shells now inching only twenty-six feet above the water, a land basically neither more nor less than a huge tidal flat. A good place for bonefish.

It is also a good place to sink a boat. The island is nearly surrounded by the most dangerous coral reef in the Caribbean—if statistics can be believed—for it is littered with the bleached skeletons of more shipwrecks than any other in the arc of islands stretching from the Florida Keys to Venezuela. Shipwrecks (like grizzly bears) can help keep a wilderness in character, and only 120 full-time inhabitants now populate the twenty square miles of this island. The developers and cruise ships haven't made it this far. It's too dangerous.

Much of the shoreline remains in a near natural state. Mangroves. Dunes. Cactus and thorny scrub. It is a harsh, desert land where life is dependent on the fresh water found only briefly during and after the intermittent rains, and in the faint light of the morning star as we bashed through the waves, it was desolation so beautiful it made me feel like dancing.

"Bonefish don't need no steenking condos," I yelled over the wind.

Duke nodded. He knew what I was thinking. Bonefish grew up in the family of the most primitive of living fish with hard skeletons, and shared the seas with the last of the dinosaurs. We bounced along through a tropical land in many ways similar to the Montana of 250 million years ago, when the Madison Limestone was forming.

Perhaps, even now, I wondered, the rich mineral veins of the next Montana were being formed in the volcano beneath the boat. Perhaps, in the next Gondawana-like shift of the continental plates, Africa and South America would re-join, pushing the accumulated rock layers in this shallow sea into high cliffs sheltering a mountain trout river full of futuristic stone flies, and someone would find the gold, and put in a mine, and maybe kill the bugs first then the trout.

That's Ju-Ju. What comes around in the cosmic cycle, goes around. You can run, but you can't hide. Find the underlying patterns to life, and you'll catch more fish. Understand the patterns, and you'll have more fun. Happiness is the insight that comes from accepting your place in the circle of life.

Some days it all seems so clear; for me, those moments of clarity come only when I am as far into the wilderness as I can get. I was on the very brink of understanding that blue-sky morning when Garfield suddenly threw the wheel to the right. I was hurled against the bulkhead, and the boat swerved sharply toward the deeper water.

Garfield pointed and called, "Mud mon."

"My God," said the Duke. "My God." He grabbed up his rod. "It must be a quarter of a mile long."

I stared wildly at the ocean. My moment of clarity was utterly gone. I didn't see a thing.

Bonefish, at times, feed in large schools, sucking water through their gills and snorting it through their mouths, blasting holes in the sand, then digging with body and tail down after crabs and shrimp and clams like a herd of piscine Rototillers. The silt they kick up creates what is known in bonefishing vernacular as a "mud," and the experts call it easy fishing.

That much, I knew.

It sounded good in the book, but out here in the ocean — in bonefish central — it wasn't easy at all. I couldn't even *find* a mud that was supposedly as long as a city block. Garfield cut the engine and we drifted in the swells. I searched frantically for the phantom mud. The Duke was now casting hard into the wind. I had absolutely no idea what I was supposed to be doing.

"Where the hell is the mud," I shouted.

"We be in de mud mon."

"We're IN the mud?" I was about to panic. "We ARE?" I wanted to catch a bonefish so badly that I was leaping up and down with excitement. "I don't see a thing!" I screamed over the wind.

Garfield smiled. "No worries. Jus' cas' mon."

I ripped line from my reel. We cast furiously from the pitching boat, hurtling before the wind, blown so fast that even the heaviest of our flies had no chance of getting down to the bottom feeding bonefish.

"It's too deep," yelled the Duke, "We need sinking lines."

In the next instant the dark green water filled with the quicksilver of flashing fish. "Jocks! Strip fas' mon. Dey fight good ass all bad hell."

We were into a school of jacks, blue runners, predators feeding on bait fish, which in turn were feeding on the muddy smorgasbord of the sea now being served up by the rooting bonefish. Garfield jerked his lure back in quick bursts. A blue runner smashed his epoxy bonefish fly. He set the spinning rod in a holder in the gunwale, the fish still on, slashing, attracting other jacks within casting distance of our flies.

We sailed through the mud three times, shake-and-bake streamer fishing for jacks up to about two pounds, no bones about it, biding our time, waiting for Garfield's sixth sense to tell him—on this particular day—when the bonefish would begin feeding on the flats. The sun was well off the horizon and the tide was coming when Garfield said: "Dis coul' be de time."

He opened the throttle wide, and the boat fishtailed through a tight figure eight over the school of mudding fish. "Godda be makin' dem fishes to movin'," he explained, then as he turned the boat toward shore he ordered, "Siddown now, mon."

A few minutes of racing and the green water went white. The water was only a few feet deep when Garfield cut the motor, and held a finger to his lips. He poled quietly through the shallows, and slipped the anchor over the side. A pair of black-tipped sharks swam past, every few feet leaving swirls of sand as their tails swept the bottom like brooms.

"What fly should I use," I asked, not thinking about sharks as long as my leg.

"Try dis firs'." Garfield handed me a fly about two inches long, with a gold mylar body, orange marabou tail, soft grizzly hackle wings, and a long tuft of white bucktail.

I looked it over uncertainly. "What is it?"

"De bonefish special." It did not look like much of anything I would have expected to swim by my feet, but then, a royal wulff does not look like any mayfly I have ever seen either. When in doubt: don't argue with the guide. I tied on the special.

"Spread ou' mon," said Garfield. We scattered, Duke and I on either side of Garfield. "Now slow walk wid de current, bit fasser den de tide, den dose fishes don' smell troubles til too domn late for dem."

We began walking. There is nothing—not friends, not books, not lawyers, guns, or money—nothing that can prepare you for this moment when you realize a dream, for this moment when you first stalk a flat scanning for bonefish. Every nerve ending is completely alive, and you are awash in the beauty. It is an incredible experience. There is nothing that can prepare you for this moment because bonefish in the water, for all intents and purposes, are invisible.

"Dere dey are mon," hissed Garfield, pointing, "Two tree dozen bones righ' dere."

I strained to see in the surface glare, but came up empty.

"Got 'em," said Duke.

Where? Damn it, Where! I still didn't see anything that could possibly be a fish.

Duke was leaning hard forward, bent at the waist, peering intently at the water. He false cast once, twice, and shot line out into the blankness of the sea. Duke stripped in line slowly, then stood up and said, "They were too far away."

"Goddom fish. Dey turn bad scare."

"Did they smell us?"

"No mon, dat dere coul' be de scare bird." He pointed to the dark shadow on the bright water of a low-flying seagull.

The Duke nodded his assent. "So, what do you think? About twenty fish in that school?"

"Yah mon, bout dot."

"All right." The Duke took a deep breath. "That was fun. Let's go find some more."

Twenty bonefish? Where? Where!

We turned, and started slowly down the flat. I looked as I had never looked before, thinking, *I want a fish so bad,* turning each little clump of turtle grass into a fish, each little sparkle in each little wave into a fish, thinking, *this is fishy water,* pulse racing, staring into the glint and the glare and the ripples in the sand until I was adrift in the shimmering reflections, mesmerized, an unlit powder keg of nerves with a short fuse.

Garfield tapped me on the shoulder. "Dere dey are mon," he hissed.

I'll admit it. I was a mite startled when he unexpectedly slipped up behind me and lit the fuse.

"Don' jump mon!" Garfield grunted under his breath. "Cas'! Now!"

"Cast?" I wondered if my hair had turned white. "Where! I haven't seen a fish yet."

"Jus' cas' mon, hurry now."

He pointed. I eyeballed the angle of his arm, and flopped out a cast.

"Good mon. Jus' wait. O.K. mon, strip slow, strip slow. Stop now. Stop. Dey chase it."

"Oh," I thought suddenly calm, "so those are bonefish."

I had the strip, but not the stop, and seven bonefish had materialized at my feet. A fish followed my fly, watching it creeping through the sand, the fly now so close that my tippet was in the rod guides. I froze, crouched low with my butt on the bottom, my breath caught up in my throat. The bonefish that had been following my fly then turned away; and swam confidently past like I was just another errant mangrove. When the last fish passed, I turned to cast. The bonefish caught the movement, and the school vanished like a puff of smoke in a strong wind.

The entire episode—from first sighting to final disappearance—had taken only a few moments. These fish give you as much of a chance to present a fly as lightning gives you to leap aside; and at times, the cast to an approaching bonefish happens so quickly that it doesn't seem as if it happened at all.

"What h-h-happened?" I sputtered. It was so fast: There had been no time to think.

Garfield just smiled, ear to ear, a huge goofy grin with his big red tongue flopped to the side, shrugging wide with open shoulders and outstretched arms, a grin that started in the soles of his feet and ended in the roots of his hair.

It was a great grin worth a thousand words, a shrug every guide should master, a grin explaining why in the same feeding lane some trout will take a nymph, some a pupae, and others only a #23 spent-wing midge tied on a hook hand forged in Kenya just after sunrise on the winter solstice.

"There are some things," said the grin, "that just are."

I took a deep breath. Now that it was over, I was twitching like a puppet on a string. I took another long, deep breath, and exhaled slowly. "Did the bonefish take the f-fly?" I asked.

"No, mon, not dis time," said Garfield.

"Should I switch flies?"

"Coul' be, mon, but better you don' move de fly so fas'. De bait he don' outrun de fish—de bait he try hide quick bury in de san'."

Bones so close, I thought, *I could have touched them.* I swallowed hard to get my heart out of my mouth. Garfield was probably right, but as I looked at the fly, it just didn't feel right, and if you can't fish with confidence, you can't catch fish.

"Garfield," I said, "I have a feeling."

He nodded. "Goddom right. I see dat by da way you jump."

I was hearing from a familiar friend. The animal within (that bundle of fur hidden deep in our most ancient web of nerves that can still sniff the evening wind for an approaching storm) was calling out. That little voice of intuition has often been all that stood between me, a day of fishing, and a skunk dinner—when the animal calls, I answer.

"Tell me mon," said Garfield, "Wot you t'inking 'bout?"

"I think we should match the hatch," I replied. Throughout the morning small brown crabs had been scuttling about the bottom, disappearing in tiny puffs of sand as we drew near. Bonefish eat lots of crabs, up to nearly half of their diet according to some studies.

I tied on a McCrab. Originally designed as a permit fly, the McCrab is a realistic imitation of a crab, with legs of knotted rubber bands and bead-chain eyes. It is also heavy with lead and bulky with clipped deer hair, and even under the best of conditions it casts about as well as a carburetor.

Garfield eyed the heavy fly doubtfully.

"You cas' dat beeg t'ing in dis wind?"

"It won't be pretty, but I can do it."

"You try dat cas' firs'."

"Here goes," I said, and hauled a hard back cast into the wind. I leaned into the forward cast, putting everything I had into it, powering forward to shoot as much line as possible, painting a long, wide casting stroke then snapping with my whole body as the loop unrolled.

Garfield whistled, long and low.

"You right. Dat not pretty."

I could only groan.

"You bleedin'." Garfield shook his head.

I had been knocked nearly senseless. The speeding crab took me smack-dab in the center of the soft spot at the top of the brain stem in the back of my head. I fought nausea and swayed in place, gathering courage for another cast, finally trying a modified roll cast with a tail wind assist.

"Dat good 'nough mon," shrugged Garfield.

I shook my head. Good enough seemed too generous a description. "You think so?"

"What I really t'ink is bes' you don' kill you dead dis fine day."

We turned and resumed our slow stalk. The wind, the tide, and the sun were all to our backs. With the sun well up and behind us, the task of spotting fish would never be easier. Even so, that did not mean it was easy. You have to remember that to a beginner bonefish are invisible, and only occasionally reveal themselves in one of several ways.

The best is the silver flash of tailing fish, when the sun sparkles on the translucent tails of feeding fish in shallow water. Tailing fish are generally the easiest to see, and since they are preoccupied with feeding, also the easiest to approach and catch. Tailing fish are an avid bonefisherman's wet dream.

Sometimes there will be nervous water, water that is somehow different, water that bulges or moves or flattens or chops or vees. It is a mirage, a piece in a wet, sandy puzzle that is oddly out of place. It is as much a feeling as a vision—like nymph fishing for trout.

Sometimes in bright sunlight you will see the dark shadows of bonefish flitting across a sandy bottom, once in a while you might actually see a fish. Usually a first-time bonefisherman won't see any of this, and nothing is all I had seen when Garfield again whistled low under his breath.

He pointed urgently with both hands at the water dead ahead. Duke looked. He saw. He cast. I still hadn't seen any fish, but I was getting used to it. I flipped my line up and out, and then the loudest sound on the flat was the Duke's reel screaming as a hooked bonefish raced for safety. In the time it took for me to look up at Duke his fish was already the length of the fly line away.

"He take it mon," hissed Garfield.

"I know," I said, "Look at all the backing that fish pulled off! And he hasn't even slowed down yet."

"NO MON! YOU!"

"Me?" I thought. I turned to where my line was moving slowly upstream into the current. It had to be a fish. I set the hook with a hard strip strike. It came up solid. I had done it! And I hadn't even seen it. Whatever 'it' was.

The hooked fish darted in tiny circles, staying with the school, not yet quite sure what the problem was. I cleared the line, all ready for the run. I couldn't wait for that legendary bonefish run. Then my line went slack. "No, No, NO!" I yelled. "What happened?"

Garfield scratched his chest and looked at the sky. "He don' have it good."

I pulled in my line, and checked the hook. "It's still sharp. What went wrong?"

"Coul' be dat fly domn beeg. Bonefish got de tiny mouth."

"Is it too big for bones? Should I change it?"

"Mebbe not dis day. Dem fishes was after dat crab fly."

"I don't have any smaller crabs."

"Maybe jus' pop dem bones. Hit dem harder de nex' time."

"O.K. mon." We waited for the Duke to land his fish. It was enormous.

"Maybe eight pounds," he said, holding the fish out as I snapped the obligatory hero shot with my camera. "Wow. These are Big Fish you have here Garfield."

The Duke released that bone in the shallow water, and then another, before we worked our way back to the boat and the next flat at the head end of a long sand spit. Here, the bottom was rough with hummocks, and spotted with clumps of coral and undulating turtle grass. The mottled reflections would make finding the fish that much more difficult.

"Now how am I going to see these fish?" I asked. There was frustration in my voice.

"No worries mon," replied Garfield. "I coul' be you eyes."

We slipped overboard, walking the ridge of the flat, calf deep in the shallowest of the water. Garfield had the midas touch on this day: We found fish everywhere he stopped, and it could not have been more than two minutes before his shrill whistle cut through the wind. I followed his pointing finger, and for the first time I saw — off to the side and already nearly past me — four dark shadows.

"Ai-i-i-i," cried Garfield.

I had changed casting directions to put the fly ahead of the advancing fish. The back cast was closer to the guide than the forward cast to the fish, but it didn't seem to matter, because as soon as the fly hit the water the bonefish jostled each other in a leisurely race toward a crab dinner. I stripped the fly back in slow bursts. A coil of line hung down into the water from the rod. I had pulled in ten feet of line when I finally felt the take.

"Remember, mon," whispered Garfield. "Pop 'im good."

The line tightened as the bonefish swam away. I counted one, two and hit the fish like I was skid-and-release woolly bugger fishing on 1x for autumn brown trout. I wanted that hook to pierce deep into that bony mouth. I wanted that fish to know who was boss.

I never was very good at upper level management. One nanosecond later the dilithium crystals glowed as the bonefish went into warp drive. The line whistled as it exploded from the water, leaving a wide arc of spray glistening in the sun. The slack was whipped into a loop that lassoed the tail piece of the rod as it shot past, and the line twanged to an abrupt halt.

Something had to give. It wasn't the fish.

"Hey, wot hoppen?" said Garfield as the line went slack.

"The leader snapped." I held up the rod, and loosened the loop of line from the butt.

Garfield shook his head. "I tole you, you won' stop dese fishes."

"That's three strikes," I thought, wondering if that meant I was out as we trudged back to the boat through the chop. "Damn," I said. "Damn!"

"O.K. my frien'," said Garfield, looking over at me in his yellow shirt. "One other chance dis fine morn' you get."

It was the last chance before Africa, at the east end of the island, where centuries of pounding waves from the Atlantic Ocean have dumped out a long shallow shoal of broken coral. The square bulk of a wrecked freighter squats firmly on the nearby reef, just past the two rounded piles of empty pink conch shells, tens of thousands of shells discarded by commercial divers, rising now since the last hurricane in huge mounds like pink breasts each the size of a Trailways bus from the sea.

We cruised through the deeper aquamarine water between the symmetrical breasts and the shoal, just off the foaming white seam delineating the edge of the dark olive flat. We rounded the point of the island into the wind, and the waves were larger: so much larger that the largest of the waves began breaking over the bow into the open boat.

"Dere dey are," called Garfield.

We jumped up. At least one hundred bonefish were gliding through the shallows along the edge of the flat. You couldn't miss them from our perch high in the boat. Garfield raced past the fish, and water now poured in over the bow as we crashed through the waves.

"Where's the bail bucket," I yelled. Garfield just laughed.

"No worries. You get dat fish now. We cut dem off at de pass," he yelled back, John Wayne in dreadlocks, a testament to the power of satellite television and the New World culture.

We wallowed in the surf as Garfield cut the engine. Three-foot high waves crashed about us on the shoal. Duke crouched in the bow, rod in hand, poised for a leap into the shallow water just beyond the breaking waves. The wind and the surf roared. We surged past jagged heads of living coral, and Garfield dropped the anchor. Literally.

"Bad t'ing, mon," he cried, "De rope loose."

The loop at the end of the anchor rope had pulled free from the stanchion. There was nothing now to hold us back, and we were driven quickly out of control toward the jagged shoal.

"Here they come," said the Duke, who had never taken his eyes off the fish. He was focused, in the zone, ready to catch his fourth bonefish of the morning, and completely unaware we were about to become the latest in a long line of shipwrecks on the island.

"Jump Mon," cried Garfield, and the Duke leaped for the foaming line of surf at the edge of the flat. He came up just short, and crashed down on a coral head jutting up from the deeper water.

There is something you should know about the Duke. He is a big boy. He was a pulling guard on his college football team, and was invited to training camp as a free agent by the Dolphins. When he hits something, it stays hit. The reef never stood a chance.

The fragile shell of coral burst on impact. The Duke plummeted through sea fans and staghorn, buried waist deep in living reef. The highest of the waves lapped at his chest. The fish were close, and moving fast. He was ready. He began his cast. Then he screamed.

In frustration. The sea birds had built a nest in his reel when his back was turned, and he watched, helpless, line hopelessly tangled, as at least a hundred bonefish darted past twenty feet away. He leaned forward, arms raised, fingers clenched, as if he might go after them with only his bare hands and teeth.

Meanwhile, back at the boat, I hung backwards off the bow, fending away the coral with my feet. Garfield fired up the outboard, and edged in reverse away from the crashing line of surf.

Garfield laughed again. "Jump Mon! De waves is bad here."

"Are you crazy?" I yelled, looking at the Duke in his cocoon of coral. "Get closer!"

"Dis de bes' I coul' do you."

I looked at the surf. "No way," I yelled. "Get closer!"

"Coul' be prolly you see dere more fishes. Now *hurry* mon!"

More fish. Some things you do because you want to, and some things you do because you have to. I jumped, rod held high, out into the deep blue water, and hoped for the best. A curling wave snatched me up like driftwood, then dropped me gently on the flat and ebbed away.

"Huh," I thought. I put my hat back on. "That was easy."

"Fish down to de conch pile," yelled Garfield over the roar of the Evinrude as he sped away.

Duke had clambered from his hole, and was inspecting himself for damages. "Not a scratch," he said, "I went straight down."

"Lucky." We watched yet another shark swim by. They were everywhere.

"I kept waiting for the pain," he said, "and it never came."

"I still can't believe you jumped."

"I didn't even stop to think about it." The Duke poured the water out of his boxes of flies, then added, "It wouldn't be the Third World, without a little adventure now and then."

"So far, so good," I agreed. "There sure seems to be a lot of fish on this island anyway."

The Duke was already looking down the flat. "Let's go find out."

We shuffled down the flat, leaving a light cloud of green silt in our wake. The sun was now off to the side, and the surface glare was much worse. It had already been a long day. The adrenaline was wearing off. The bottom shimmered like a hypnotist's crystal. My eyes were tired. I hadn't admitted it but I was done fishing, and was just walking, when the Duke whistled.

"Bones! Twelve o'clock high."

My torpor evaporated. I scanned the flat. Nothing. "Where?" "Where?"

"Just past that little mangrove twig. Tailers."

And then I saw the tails. There were four fish, cruising haphazardly about one hundred feet in front of us. All the tails were big, but one tail soared majestically above the others, gleaming huge like the sail on a silver-plated wind surfer.

Life isn't fair. Duke saw the fish, but the fish turned toward me. I was to get the cast at these fish, three large fish and then Moby, a great white whale of a bonefish, a fish that to this day remains the largest bonefish I have ever seen. And it happened on my first day of flats fishing.

That's Ju-Ju.

"Huge fish," whistled the Duke. "Take him."

And finally, for the first time that day, tuned in and turned on, I found the zone. Action, reaction, and a sweet cast later the fly dropped gently in the waves, where the surging current swung the fly just so in front of the rooting fish. The biggest fish turned like the wind on a mountain lake, his pointed tail spearing up shiny in the air as he went nose down to suck in the crab. BAM, I set the hook.

Bonefish swim, at top speed, at about thirty-five miles an hour, or fifty feet per second. Twelve seconds later that fish was two football fields away. It was a run better by at least two kilograms of purest grandeur than any other I had ever known, and in about the time it takes to pee your pants the fish had ripped out nearly all of my backing.

The fish could easily have spooled me, but he stopped in the shallow water just above the blue water trough at the end of the flat. The conch pile breasts glowed pink in the sun just across the deep channel, rising from a shallow reef that represented safe haven for the bonefish. There was just one problem with the escape route the bonefish had picked, and it had sharp teeth.

The deep blue water trough between the bonefish and the relative safety of the shell mounds was barracuda country. The bonefish was loathe to venture past the drop-off into the deeper water; because a hooked bonefish is a bonefish in trouble, and barracuda can smell trouble.

The fish held for the moment and I worked down the flat, slowly gaining lost line. I know now that I should have been running Moby down at flank speed, taking backing as quickly as possible, but I was in a daze, blown away like dust by the power of that first run.

Therefore I wasn't anything even remotely resembling ready when the fish blitzed down into the deeper water, run number two, a moving target intent on escape, every second fifty feet closer to the conch piles.

"He'll cut the line on the coral," I yelled. I tried to stop him, and palmed the reel. It was like trying to stop a bull elk with a band-aid. Pop, just like that, the fish was gone. I crumbled butt first to the bottom of the sea. Sitting head in hands, sea salt burning my chapped lips, I stared into the shiny water. The waves lapped at my armpits, and mud oozed into my shorts as I sunk deep into a well of abject dejection. The Duke came over, fingering at the collar of his XXL T-shirt.

"I farmed him," I mumbled. "I can't believe I farmed him."

"Your learning curve," he said, "was steep today."

"What a fish," I cursed softly to the sand.

Garfield roared up, ready to take us back to camp.

"Goddom it," he yelled, "I tole you. You can't stop dese fishes."

"Goddom it yourself," I mumbled down into the waves.

"You need a beer," said the Duke, looking down to where I sat in the mud. "Bad."

COCKTAIL HOUR

When you need a beer, bad, you don't want anything to get in your way. Fortunately, it was downwind all the way back to camp; more importantly, we were camped beside a bar.

"I'm buying," I said when we pulled up to the dock.

We walked the fifty feet to Neptune's Treasure, and sat at a round table on the stone veranda, in the cool shade of a grove of coconut trees. Beers and mixed drinks were an American dollar, we kept a tab, and poured our own on the honor system. The ocean lapped at our feet. Palm fronds rustled in the languid sea breeze. Sailboats swayed in the chop.

Just as there are times to drink and times to drink too much, there are places to drink and places to drink too much. We were in the right place at the right time.

"Now, this," said the Duke, toasting the azure sky with iced gin and olives, "is camping."

"Happy birthday," I said. I leaned on the beat-up guitar I had borrowed.

"Feliz cumpleaños a tú," sang Juaníta, Gloria, y María, the singing sisters of San Juan, in the tight three-part harmony that only family does best.

The girls were off-duty lounge lizards, cruise ship entertainment for the blue hair and polyester crowd, and as far away from the luxury liners as they could get in one day. They were on vacation. It showed.

"It you birt'day?" asked Garfield, "How man'?"

"Forty-seven," lied the Duke.

"Tell you wha'." Garfield smiled at the girls and stood up. "I come back later, we go into town for birt'day party."

Garfield left, and the singing sisters went to get ready for dinner. I just couldn't sit still. I exchanged the guitar for a pair of pliers and a knife, and began prying on the end cap of the reel seat on my brand new saltwater fly rod.

The Duke looked over. "What are you doing?" he asked.

"This end cap is stuck." I gave the seat a vigorous twist. "I couldn't get my fighting butt in today." I squeezed the pliers and gave a mighty yank. "These fish are so big I'm going to need it."

The Duke looked puzzled. "Those end caps just pop off," he said. "It shouldn't take a pair of pliers."

"Finally," I replied. "There it comes," and with one last jerk,

I wrenched free the end cap. Jagged chunks of coca-bola wood and hardened glue clung to the metal. Something was wrong. Very wrong.

"Hey," said the Duke. "That's my rod."

Uh-oh. Same case, different rod. I had been using Duke's six weight instead of my eight, and I had just ripped off the end of his reel seat. Even by the standards I set for myself, this was pretty stupid. I couldn't believe it—all morning I had been casting carburetors in a typhoon with a six weight noodle of a rod.

"Send me a bill," I said. "What can I say but I'm sorry."

At least the Duke understood what I was going through. This wasn't his first rodeo. "The needle," he replied, "went in deep for you today."

I nodded. He had hit the nail right on the head. I was trembling, beside myself with excitement, only partially aware of my surroundings, newly addicted to a sport that is as habit forming as cocaine, and way more expensive. I was hooked. I was a bonefish junkie.

"Now," I said, "I'm going to have to get a job."

"Good luck." Duke bent low to light a cigarette in the wind. "Just promise me one thing."

"What's that?"

"Don't try and fix any more of my fly rods."

And then, after a dinner of fresh swordfish, it was Saturday night in the islands. We rode with the girls in the back of an open pickup, over sea shell roads, through the dark of a new moon, to the only village on the island, next stop oblivion.

"Dat de Banana Well," called Garfield. The stick walls of the only dance hall in town bulged in and out under the deafening beat of steel drum music. A six-foot fluorescent banana glowed yellow above the door. We walked in to one of the all-time great bar scenes.

The wet air dripped with the musk of sweaty dancers. The pungent smell of exotic spices—of nutmeg and cinnamon and myrrh—hung in the air. So did an inflatable Budweiser blimp, grey, red, and slightly flaccid, dangling from the grass-thatched ceiling and festooned with blinking Christmas lights. A chaotic potpourri of sailors from their boats, and dark natives with flashing gold teeth and great round hoop earrings, were dancing up a white and African fury.

A thin young black man approached us, then lashed out with his right fist. Garfield quickly punched back, then they gently rubbed outstretched fists top together to bottom in the local variation on a handshake.

"De welcome coul' be fo' you mon," said the boy.

"Dis be Carlos," said Garfield, and introduced us all around, explaining that Carlos owned the bar. Sort of. Actually it was his father's bar, but his father was off island on a buying trip, and Junior was pouring a lot of free drinks.

Carlos leaned close above the din of music. "You one dem movie star?" he shouted.

"Me?" I pointed to the center of my chest. "In the movies?" I shook my head no.

"T'ing is mon you coul' be de look alike Don Johnson," Carlos said, and rubbed his chin.

I rubbed my own chin, which I had just shaved for the first time in twenty years as part of a Halloween costume. I sported a five-day stubble, but any similarity I had to *Miami Vice* reruns ended right there. It was ridiculous. I look like a movie star like a rabbit looks like a gorilla.

"Not me," I yelled back. I had to laugh.

"Oh." Carlos smiled at me. "I thought maybe coul' be you wid de beach movie mon."

"Movie?" I accepted the cold beer Carlos offered. "What movie?"

Carlos said it wasn't really a movie so much as a commercial, and it was being filmed by a Dutch cruise line. The film crew, knowing that sex sells, hoping to tantalize the folks back home in Amsterdam into a cruise, had been throwing money all over the island building a sea-shell-encrusted shower stall. The shower stall was open to the sea breeze from the waist up; when the cameras finally rolled the stall was to be full of naked actresses showering together against a tropical backdrop of sand, sea, and sky.

"Dat be one dem girls dere," Carlos said, pointing into the corner where your basic blonde Norse Goddess in a halter top lounged with one shoulder against a wall.

"Is that right?" I said, wondering if there were any bonefish flats in the vicinity of where the filming would occur, knowing it didn't matter: I'd fish there anyway.

"Well, coul' be mon wid dat face you fin' de work in de movies." Carlos waved a thin arm at the bartender and bought me another drink.

"I doubt it," I said, "But thanks." I didn't mind small talking the man who was buying, but I'd heard enough about my face. To change the subject, I asked, "Have you lived here all your life?"

"Now dat be de sad question." Carlos looked at his feet. "I be borned on de island, but leave soon jus' de tiny babe."

"You want to talk about it?" It was a rhetorical question. Carlos wore his heart on his sleeve, and it was clear that he wanted to talk. Carlos looked up, and immediately launched into a tale of faded love.

Carlos said his mother left his father when Carlos was too young to remember—when he was a baby not yet two years old. His mother took Carlos to Brazil, and remarried. His mother's new husband had raised Carlos as his own son for over twenty years, and nothing had ever been said to Carlos about his real father.

And then, about six months ago, Carlos and his mother had climbed aboard a bus in downtown Rio. On the back wall of the bus was a four-color glossy poster of a smiling man waist deep in the ocean, holding up a lobster in each hand, advertising a string of Caribbean islands. His mother had seen the poster and shrieked out loud.

"I know the picture," I said. I had seen it on the cover of a travel brochure: The happy black man, his wriggling red lobsters, the blue sea, and the blue sky comprised the quintessential celluloid portrait of everything a vacation in the islands was supposed to be.

"Dat man," mother told son, pointing at the poster, "Dat be you daddy true now back den."

The devout Catholic in his mother saw the picture not as an advertising photograph so good it had to be used, but rather as a sign from Jesus, and then, in the back seat of the bus, after all those years, in a tear-soaked confessional, the whole story of Carlos's true father finally came out. Carlos had come back to the islands to meet his biological father, and was now working the bar his father owned.

"So how do you and your father get along now?" I asked.

"Hey, not so bad. But be big differen' mon."

"I'll bet."

"Hey, how 'bout now some pizza? Coul' be cook up good in de house of mine?"

"No thanks." I politely declined. Carlos was kind of weird, and besides, I wanted to dance. "I'm just not hungry," I added.

I wandered away into the crowd. "Hey, wot Carlos want mon?" said Garfield, when I caught up to him.

"Nothing really." I shrugged. "He just wanted to talk. He said I look like Don Johnson."

Garfield laughed and said, "Dat be good bet. Bes' you know dat boy like boys."

"What?" Recognition dawned in my eyes. That was it. Carlos had been hitting on me. "He's gay?"

"You got all dat right boss."

I considered the ramifications of being gay on an island of 120 people. I didn't envy Carlos his life. One thing was certain: "I'm sure glad I didn't go out for pizza," I said.

The Duke was busy waxing all comers at the pool table out on the porch; Garfield and I looked around for the singing sisters of San Juan. It was a great party. We danced. We sang. We poured down the hut specialty—a vicious blend of rum, kahlua, and pineapple/coconut/papaya juice—by the pint. It is not a drink for the faint of heart, and later I melted down next to Juanita in the fresh air outside by the pool table.

"Chew gonna faint?" She poked me with her index finger.

"I hope not." But then there was really no way of telling what a man high on the hut specialty was capable of.

"¿Que haces aquí?" said the woman on my left. "What are you doing here?"

She was from Colombia, traveling the Caribbean by sailboat with her husband, who was now juggling a pineapple, an orange, and a foil bag of potato chips under a palm tree by the rusted-out hulk of a car balanced on broken cinder blocks.

"Yo soy pescador," I replied, making casting motions with my free arm, the one that was not resting lightly across Juaníta's brown shoulders.

"A feeshermon, como Jesús, ¿No?" said Juaníta, digging a sharp elbow into my side. She had heard quite enough fish stories for one night, thank you very much, and was not in the least bit thrilled with the turn of the conversation. She didn't seem to mind the arm.

"¿Quieres sacar los sabalos?" said Miss Colombia.

"Tarpon?" That got my attention. "¿Dónde?"

"¿Sabalos?" The Duke, radar on, flaps up, zeroed in from twenty feet away. Sabalos was one of the few Spanish words he knew, but he knew it well. He took three giant steps still holding his pool cue and grabbed my arm. "Where?" he said, "Find out where."

I established, in pidgin Spanish, that Miss Colombia had been seeing tarpon at the government pier nearly every night at low tide.

"It's low tide now," said the Duke.

"It's three in the morning," I replied.

"Are you coming or not?"

Talk about a tough decision. It was a question of priorities, and while there aren't many native girls in Montana, there simply aren't *any* tarpon. "Juaníta," I said, "I have to go."

"Wot, chew nuts?" Juaníta leaped up, her dark eyes livid.

I didn't answer Juaníta one way or the other, because the truth is, I'm not sure.

TARPON

We gave an old man five dollars for a ride back to camp, and grabbed our fishing tackle. A bit later the night sky was black and getting blacker as we lurched down the beach toward the government pier. "There go the stars," I said.

It was the end of hurricane season. Short-lived but intense squalls blew in sporadically, mostly at night, and now the clouds covered first Orion then the Pleiades. Lightning flashed, thunder boomed, and rain began to pelt down. We were on a rocky point exposed to the full fury of the storm.

"Better run for that shack." Duke pointed to a storage shed at the end of the pier. He got there first, and shook the door. "It's locked," he yelled.

We huddled on the lee side of the ramshackle building, out of the wind, but not quite out of the torrent of rain cascading off the roof. We pressed hard against the splintered planks as if trying to back away from the bullets of a firing squad, but every so often, just when it was least expected, a cold ball of water the size of a thumb would swing in and detonate in an open eye.

It was a cold, wet, Hailie Selassie version of Chinese water torture, and I cringed, waiting for the next explosion, thinking of warm Juaníta, wondering just exactly what in the hell had possessed me to leave beautiful Puerto Rico to go fishing in the rain three hours before dawn.

"Don't think about it," said the Duke.

I've never quite gotten used to the fact that the Duke can read my mind. I think it has something to do with the fact that he catches so many fish. "I can't help it," I replied.

"Think about tarpon."

"I'm thinking about wild geese. As in a chase. This is crazy."

The storm relented as quickly as it had begun. While Duke rigged with eighteen inches of sixty-pound shock tippet, and a bright orange bullet-headed fly, I strolled down to the water, where two silhouettes with the proportions of end-to-end fifty gallon oil drums dissolved into the darkness beneath the dock.

"Tarpon!" I had never been scared of a fish before, but I was now. "They're really here!" They were so very, very big. "Tarpon!"

"Where?" The Duke bolted down. "Where?"

Duke coiled shooting line at his feet, and stood ready to make a cast with the same eight-weight rod he used to throw jig-heads at three-pound brown trout. It was the heaviest rod we owned, but it did not seem possible that such a slender wand could subdue one of the monsters I had just seen.

"Are you sure that's enough rod?" I asked.

The Duke wiped rain from his face with the sleeve of his shirt. "No," he replied, "but it came with a twenty-five-year guarantee."

"That's something anyway."

We stood shoulder to shoulder on a concrete boat-launching ramp beside the government pier, beneath a shining overhead street-light that had been installed for the convenience of sailors arriving at night. It was also convenient for tarpon fishermen: schooling bait fish had been attracted by the light, and rolling tarpon show-ed as momentary flashes of silver gleaming hot in bucket-mouthed pursuit of a late night snack. Every few minutes, from out in the darkness surrounding the small ring of light in which we stood, there was a splash like a fat man doing a cannonball off the high dive as another leaping tarpon tumbled back to the planet.

The Duke had fished for tarpon before. He said there was no point in wearing out your arm blind casting. We stared into the waves, sight fishing to foraging fish, waiting for a tarpon to show itself before making the cast. The Duke lit a cigarette. I smoked a Honduran cigar I had gotten duty-free in San Juan.

"There's one," we both cried together at a flash of silver a good sixty feet away.

The Duke double hauled directly into the teeth of the wind. The fly was bright orange, hummed as it flew, and dropped a dozen feet short. "Hmmm," said the Duke as he stripped back line until he again held the fly, "This might be tough."

I looked at the fly in his hand. It was six inches long, with lead dumbell eyes, and tied on a hook which was big and heavy enough to hang an elk quarter for butchering. I pointed at the fly and said: "Why don't you try something lighter, a fly that would be a little easier to cast?"

The Duke stretched, arched his back, then set his feet for the next cast. "It has to be heavy," he replied, "tarpon don't like to come up for a fly."

"Well, just don't let that thing hit you in the back of the head."

The Duke shuddered at the thought. "A stiffer rod would help in this wind."

"You can't have too many rods," I agreed, jabbing with my cigar for emphasis. "We need a twelve weight."

We had time to chat between casts as we waited for those beautiful gleaming flashes the size of a galvanized garbage can. The Duke grunted with the effort of a few more short, futile casts to far-out flashes, then a fish rolled, much closer, only thirty feet away. This cast was immediate and perfect, and led the tarpon like a good shot on a flushing pheasant. Mend, mend, sinking, sinking, and the bright fly became a fleeing bait fish in the tarpon's face as Duke jerked in line a foot at a time.

Thirty feet away the water erupted, and then the air was full of fish. A flying tarpon demands slack in the line, as their sharp gill rakers can easily sever a tight leader as they thrash wildly during a jump, and the Duke bowed low with the rod to give line. The tarpon smashed back down. The fish jumped, and jumped again, and then the jumps were heard rather than seen out in the darkness of the sea.

Twenty-five minutes later Duke was thigh deep in the waves, taking a pounding as the surf crashed about him on the rocks. He threw his arm out for balance, then reached down and lifted fifty pounds of tarpon to the stars, his saucer plate eyes reflecting back the silver magic of the tarpon scales. The Duke lives for moments like these: he threw back his head and howled with a primordial delight that came from so far back on his family tree it sent shivers up my spine.

"Happy birthday," I said, admiring the biggest fish I had ever seen taken on a fly rod.

The Duke released the fish, then stood up, and hopped back over the rocks. "Your turn." He handed me the rod.

"Here goes." I stood poised in the spray at the very edge of the concrete apron. "Man it's slippery."

Hard casting for maximum distance is a full body movement more akin to throwing a fastball toward home plate than dropping midges on a spring creek, and tonight, in the home opener with the Silver Kings, the pitcher's mound had been buttered with algae. I would have to be careful.

We waited. The Duke was still twitching with excitement. A tarpon flashed, so close that it was almost easy. I dropped the fly in front of the fish; the take was as subtle as having an anvil dropped on your toe. I pumped hard to the side, once, twice, driving the sharp hook deep into the bony plate of the tarpon's mouth.

The line went slack, and then the water at our feet exploded in a tossing, turning, head-shaking volcano of liquid fury. The tarpon had run directly toward us! Ten feet away, in the glare of the street light, I stared at a hundred pounds of gleaming silver tarpon that hung suspended in the air. The six-inch fly was an orange wisp lost in a bushel basket of coal-black mouth, and the tarpon stared back with a big round eye.

We were eyeball to eyeball for an instant of eternity, in that instant I lost my soul to tarpon. No other fish could compare. The tarpon crashed back into the water, so close we were soaked by the spray. Then my reel screamed like a bad starter motor, went up an octave, and the fish was in the air again.

"BOW!" screamed the excited Duke, an inch from my ear, "YOU GOTTA BOW!"

The loud shout startled me, and I slipped in the moss, and fell on my ass. Although a fall is not technically a bow, I like to think of it as such, because it put slack in the line while the fish was jumping, and the tarpon was unable to throw the hook.

I scrambled to my feet. Alcohol, adrenaline, tobacco, and the overwhelming intensity of the situation combined to shock me into that rare state of complete focus we know all too seldom. The world slowed down, and I watched from outside myself as I played that fish. I *knew* what the tarpon would do before it happened. I *knew* I would subdue that fish.

Line smoked out as the fish leaped time and again during the next two minutes, crashing down in the vastness of the dark sea. I had never felt such raw power before. If hooking a bonefish was like trying to land a Harley, this was like trying to hold back the Starship Enterprise.

And here I thought I was having fun until I looked over at the Duke. I think in another life he must have been a rock'n'roll star. He was hammering hard up the neck of his electric air guitar, a '57 Fender Stratocaster, bending out waa-waa notes so high only a dog could hear them.

"Excuse me," he sang, with feeling, "while I kiss the sky."

I don't know if it was his singing or not, but the stars began to blink out again. It was another squall. The first of the raindrops fell just as the fish jumped for the first time in twenty minutes and took off in the strongest run yet. I had already used the long length of the pier to supplement my meager supply of backing, and we were now at the very tip of the dock.

There was nowhere to hide from the tempest. Water streamed down our faces. We leaned hard into the rain to avoid being blown over, T-shirts snapping like locker room towels in the wind. It was black as a root cellar, and bright as the inside of a flashbulb when lightning unbolted the door. Through it all, the fish kept taking line.

"Duke, look," I shouted, bending close under a flash of lightning to show him the reel. The spool was bare but for a few scant wraps of backing. "There can't be more than five feet of line left."

"Crank down the drag." His sunburned face was shiny in the rain. He threw his arms up and out. "It's all you can do."

The fish strained against the new drag setting. The match-up was now dead even.

"The reel will stop him," yelled Duke, "but I don't know about the rod."

The snap, crackle, and pop of graphite fibers was audible even above the wind, the fish and the rod the very definition of dynamic equilibrium. I held tight, willing the fish to turn, and finally, much later, I had the fly line in the rod guides once again. My arms shook with fatigue—at this point I had been fighting the tarpon for over two hours and the storm was merely a wet distant memory.

"How are we going to land him?" I said. I wanted desperately to land at least one fish this long day of fishing, and it was six feet down to the water from the dock on which we stood.

"We'll have to improvise," said the Duke. He scrounged through the various piles of nautical debris in the vicinity for something that would serve as a gaff, then returned.

"Nothing," he said. "You'll just have to beach him."

I worked slowly down the dock, a few steps at a time, toward the shore and shallow water where I could land the fish. Fifteen minutes later I was nearly close enough to shore to jump down off the dock when a sullen head shake suddenly became one last burst of speed. The tarpon dove under the dock, rubbing line and leader on the barnacle encrusted pilings.

"Do something!" I yelled, reeling frantically, running backwards, taking slack.

Duke jumped up and sprinted to the fish. Weathered chunks of storm-torn concrete were strewn about the pitted surface of the pier: the Duke used them like depth charges, lifting chunk after chunk high above his head with both hands, then firing them in a fusillade down on the fish. The tarpon, gills flaring crimson in the dark water, gave one last giant lunge for the pilings, and then swam back to the relative safety of deeper water.

"Look," called the Duke. He pointed toward the open water where a red boat was once again crashing through the waves. The sun was already a glowing sphere barely above the horizon: it was Garfield, right on time for another day of bonefishing.

"Try and flag him down," I said. "I don't think he sees us."

"It's been a long day of fishing, hasn't it?"

"That's for sure," I called back over my shoulder. "Garfield won't believe it when we tell him what happened."

I was now fifty feet from the dock, knee deep in the shallow water. The tarpon was only twenty feet away, rolling silver in the dawn's early light. I was moments away from releasing that magnificent fish when my rod gave a tremendous jerk, and was nearly yanked from my palsied hand. The line went slack.

"He's gone?" I couldn't believe it. "He's gone?" The fish couldn't be gone. Not after all that. My shoulders sagged as I turned to look back at Duke. "What happened?" I asked.

The Duke was pointing into the surf line behind me, jabbing with both arms. His mouth was moving but no words were coming out. I turned around to see what he was so worked up about, and there, twenty feet away, a triangular black fin carved the water above a black shadow the size of a canoe with five rows of teeth. The Duke finally forced enough air into his lungs to belatedly shout: "SHARK!"

At that point I was so frightened I became the first person in 2,000 years to successfully walk on water. Moments later when I was back on dry land the Duke stared at me with big, round eyes and said, "That was way too close."

I was hyperventilating. "Nuh hun nuh muh nuh ha!" I agreed.

The big hammerhead—with one bite—had sliced the tarpon completely in half. One gleaming chunk of tarpon floated slowly out with the tide. The other slab rocked slowly from side to side, churning in the small white breakers at the edge of the flat as the shark ripped at the carcass, and the water stained red the color of blood in the sunrise.

I felt bad about the tarpon. Really bad. But not as bad as I would have felt in another minute or so, when my hand would have been on the fly in the tarpon's mouth, and the shark would have eaten me too. It had been the most exciting day of fishing of my life, and I hadn't landed a fish.

That's Ju-Ju.

New-Age Sensitive Angler

THE DOMESTIC Tranquility Index (or D.T.I.) is a measure of marital bliss. It is the single most important factor in determining how many fish you will catch over the course of your lifetime, because it determines whether or not you will even be allowed out of the house. D.T.I. is a function of time—which is the same as not enough time—and is best summed up by the following exchange:

Q: "Is it possible to be both a good flyfisherman and a good golfer?"

A: "Not and stay married."

D.T.I. is measured on a sliding scale of one to ten. Forget about ten. Nobody I know ever got above a seven. At the other end of the scale, a D.T.I. of zero is defined as ten minutes of screaming followed by two days of silence. And negative numbers are possible, as in:

Q: "Want to go fishing? I hear the salmonflies are busting out on Rock Creek."

A: "I can't. My D.T.I. is off the scale."

D.T.I. isn't like money: you can't save it. It works both ways: for men and women. Consider for example that you can't build your

D.T.I. so high you'll be forgiven for an affair. You either have it or you don't. D.T.I. is a use-it-or-lose-it proposition, and as I came of age in an era of strong women and strident feminism I thought there must be a better way. Desperate times call for desperate measures; I would become a New-Age Sensitive Angler.

"That's the stupidest thing I ever heard," said each of my friends in turn when they heard my plan. "Nobody should try and teach their girlfriend how to fish."

"The couple that fishes together," I replied, "stays together."

"The couple that fishes together," they dissented, "is capable of murder in the first degree."

It was all about relationships and making them last.

My theory was that both shared passion and common goals were at the core of a successful long-term relationship. Whatever the passion in a life—be it stamp collecting, travel, or kinky videos —an appropriate partner would share it; but if that partner saw retirement as municipal bonds and condominiums at age sixty-five, where you saw sailboats and cheap rum as soon as possible, then all the common interests in the world wouldn't produce an enduring relationship.

At least that was the theory. It still seems like sage advice.

I just wish I would have followed it more often.

It was particularly difficult in the early years. My problem was lust: in the daily battle I waged with myself for bodily supremacy between common sense and even the remotest possibility of sex, raging hormones were the winner by a head every time. There were a variety of reasons for this, including the color red, for of all the hair I love red the best.

Perhaps it's my Scottish ancestry but there is something about that brightest heart-skipping shade of auburn burning against the creamy white skin of a shoulder that won't tan; about the freckles, the green eyes, and the down-like body hair; about the temper and the overflowing passion that makes my blood absolutely boil. I can't help myself.

I feel some of the same things about my favorite mayfly— *Tricorythodes minutis*, or tricos.

Once you get the minutis part, you know most of what there is to know about tricos. They are tiny, with black bodies and translucent wings, and hatch in numbers so prodigious that even the largest trout will come up to feed in water so shallow it might not even cover their backs. Trout rising to tricos will not move more than the width of their mouths from their feeding lane; casts must be as delicate as dandelion seeds drifting on the breeze, as accurate as a bullet, and above all else: drag-free. It is difficult fishing for big fish on small flies. I like the challenge. I like the incongruity. It makes my blood boil.

So you can imagine my excitement that one perfect morning in the drift boat when clouds of tricos were rising like smoke from dozens of smoldering campfires. My on-again/off-again red-headed girlfriend Jeanne was rowing; it was her first time at the oars of a fishing boat. I was fishing from the front seat. Deke, an outfitter and proprietor of the Lazy-D Flyfishing Lodge, fished from the rear. We drifted down in perfect position to the seam above the first island where a pod of rainbow trout rose with the regularity of an atomic clock.

"Get ready to drop the anchor," I whispered, "Ri-i-i-ight, now!"

"O.K." Jeanne whispered back.

But the boat never stopped. We just kept sliding right on by those huge, sipping fish.

"Quick," I yelled, "Drop the anchor!"

"Don't you yell at me," yelled Jeanne.

"Don't start arguing now," said Deke as he laid out a cast. "Be good little boyfriends and girlfriends."

"I'm not his girlfriend," sniffed Jeanne and glared at me.

"Please," I said so calmly that it hurt in the abdomen like a hernia. "Please, drop the anchor. These are very big fish and there's no wind and the bugs are up and it doesn't all come together like this but a couple days a year so please *drop the anchor.*"

"I already did," said Jeanne.

"You did?"

I spun around just in time to see the last of the anchor rope disappear off the back of the boat. I had taken it for granted that once you dropped the anchor you would know to jam the anchor rope into the cleat. It was so obvious I thought it went without saying. It was that communication thing again.

"Pull over!" I yelled. The rope and anchor together were worth over fifty dollars; I thought I could retrieve them by wading or maybe swimming.

"Don't you yell at me!" yelled Jeanne.

A trout jumped off the port bow.

"I got one," yelled Deke. Rather than worrying about things he couldn't change Deke had been fishing, and doing a big rainbow of a job of it. The fish jumped again. If you can't have fun with a pretty girl on a pretty day on a pretty river, I asked of myself, then when can you have fun? I sucked in a deep breath and turned to Jeanne.

"I'm sorry," I apologized, "I shouldn't have yelled like that. Will you be my beautiful girlfriend again so we can pull in to shore and get the anchor?"

Jeanne fingered the bone and bead earring she had made, then said, "Cut the crap."

But then, as Deke played his trout, she added, "Maybe if you're lucky."

I've always been lucky.

It's just that sometimes it's bad, and sometimes it's good.

Another girl I knew named Scary Mary had long hair so red and wonderful it glowed at the edges like a total eclipse of the sun. Mary didn't mind being called Scary because she was, but she hated, above all other things, to be called "Red." Her vehemence was such I figured it stemmed from one of those unresolved childhood issues. But the cowboy at the bar just didn't get it.

The cowboy thought he was being charming, but he had no more sense than an armadillo crossing a four-lane highway. Despite repeated warnings he finally went too far when he called her a "cute li'l carrot top."

Mary stared at the mirror behind the bar; I watched in the reflection as her eyes went cold, then began to sparkle. The cowboy was done for; I went for a pool cue in case his friends got any ideas. By the time Mary turned back to the cowboy she was wearing bedroom eyes and a toothpaste commercial smile. "O.K. Tex," she said, "you talked me into it. How about that dance you promised?"

Tex smirked to his buddies as Mary eased him off his padded imitation leather bar stool. Mary's long fingers pulled up the cowboy by his oversized silver rodeo belt buckle until his legs were spread wide against her hip: then Mary dropped back a quick half-step and hammered her knee up into his crotch. The cowboy doubled over and sucked in air against the pain; Mary picked up his beer and poured it over his head, then rapped him with the empty mug until he dropped to the floor.

"I told you," she said, "Don't ever call me Red."

You can bet I never did. And you can see what kind of women I find interesting. I think it must be one of those unresolved childhood issues.

On another day with another woman dark cumulus clouds spilled over the mountains and drizzled intermittent rain. It was November. Duke and I were fishing; Splash was rowing, her short dishwater blonde hair tucked up underneath a wool hat.

The Duke had his doubts beforehand. He had been guiding nearly every day for the last month, and now he wanted to fish, not row. "I don't know," he said. "Can your new girlfriend take her turn at the oars?"

"I think so," I said. "She's a full-time guide. She rows commercial whitewater trips all summer long, and wants to learn the fly-fishing end of things so she'll be more employable."

"Huh," said Duke, "you should open a school," but went anyway, and was glad he did.

It was one of those days when it's not quite winter and every fish in the river was up for what might be the last hatch of the season. Splash rowed first; if we weren't always in exactly the right place we were close enough that Duke and I had several doubles in only the first hour of fishing parachute blue-wing olive duns and dropper nymphs with red floss butts.

I was fishing from the back; on one of those doubles I hooked a rainbow trout that ran down and across the river and jumped over the Duke's line at the same moment his fish was jumping back toward the bank. Our lines crossed. I lowered my rod; Duke passed his rod over my line, deftly switched hands, and our lines uncrossed.

"How'd you do that?" asked Splash and laughed with delight.

"I don't know," replied Duke because it happened so fast.

Later, the same thing happened, except I was rowing. Splash was fishing the front, and Duke hooked a fish that leaped over her line on the third jump. Splash passed her rod (which was actually my rod) from hand to hand except this time she missed the hand-off. My expression could best be described as stupefied as I watched my rod float on down ahead of the boat.

"You threw my rod in the river," I said, bringing it to her attention but being careful not to yell.

The rod was now sinking slowly reel first.

"What do I do now?" Splash spoke in a stage whisper, staring downstream at the rod.

"Get it," I said through gritted teeth. "Just get it."

Splash turned and said with wide doe-in-the-crosshairs eyes, "I know, but how?"

"Get it." I said. "Just get it!"

I was a little pop-eyed myself.

The rod was a new Winston, and it was the first real dry fly rod I had ever owned. It cost as much as a month on the beach in Mexico, and was so new that this was only the second time I had used it. The rod bounced downstream; Splash leaned hard forward and I heaved on the oars playing catch-up. Ten seconds later the rod was almost within reach but nearly too deep to grab when to my astonishment Splash suddenly tensed then leaped into the cold November river.

"Now there's something you don't see every day," said the Duke.

From the expression on her face when she surfaced Splash was as surprised as anyone at what she had done. The water was so deep it floated her hat, so cold her lips turned blue, and now you know how she earned her nickname.

"Agh-h-h," gasped Splash, the air knocked from her chest, her boat-woman biceps bulging through her wet shirt as she thrashed to shore, but smiling with the rod held triumphantly skyward.

"Let's go fishing!" she yelled when she had her breath back.

"You didn't have to jump, you know," I said later, solicitous in my role as a new-age sensitive angler as we pooled clothes to come up with one dry, warm set. I have to admit I was impressed with a girl who wouldn't let a little thing like jumping in a cold river interfere with a good day of fishing.

"What was I going to do?" she replied. "You just kept shouting. Get It. Get It."

"I know, but I didn't think you'd jump out of the boat."

"Neither did I," she said looking bewildered. "It must be love."

Love is easy, especially in the beginning of a relationship.

It's the commitment that's tough.

The first several months of a new relationship are easy. Everything is new and interesting. Differences in taste and opinion seem trifling: Personal idiosyncrasies that will later have you gnashing your teeth are still viewed as adorable little quirks. All the stories are fresh and exciting. So is the sex. I realized only belatedly as I drifted through life that I had become addicted to that earliest stage of relationships: I was hooked on honeymoons.

It was at least partly a sign of the times.

I grew up in the Golden Age of promiscuity along with the just-say-yes generation. Love was just a kiss away. Orgies were in, abstinence was out. Birth control was readily available. Sexually transmitted diseases were rare and treatable. For a time it seemed as if willing and fascinating women (each perfect in her own special way) were everywhere.

For me, it was the same way with rivers. Each river was unique, and I wanted to experience them all. Like women, the rivers were beautiful and moody, tumultuous and serene, constantly changing. In trying to understand them, I lost myself to the point of thinking of nothing else, and every day held another surprise.

On one of those days Duke, Airbrush, and I had already towed an inflated raft on a trailer two hundred miles to three different rivers and it was barely noon. We had yet to wet a line. The wind was so powerful it blew a double-weighted woolly bugger from the palm of my hand: too strong for good fishing, but just right for a road trip. The back seat stunk of spilled ether from the raft repair kit, and beer cans littered the floor.

We were on our way from the Jefferson to our fourth river of the day—the Big Hole. This necessitates a run through Butte, a town for nearly a century described as the biggest mining camp on earth. Vigorous men from Ireland, China, and most countries in between worked the mines, bars, and brothels three shifts a day until the boom finally went bust; now Butte is well on its way to becoming the world's largest ghost town. Such a place has charms all its own, but still, it was for reasons known only to himself that Duke swerved onto the exit ramp for Butte, America.

"Where you goin'?" said Airbrush. "We gonna fish the Pit?"

What a thought. You might as well fish a vat of acid.

The Berkeley Pit is the eighth wonder of the world. Once a tree-covered mountain of low-grade copper ore, the Pit is now an abandoned strip mine that is rapidly becoming a toxic lake. The crater is a mile wide, a mile deep, and half full of pumpkin-colored water laden with heavy metals and a whipped topping of wind-blown foam. The Pit graces the center of uptown Butte like the hole in a doughnut, if the doughnut was glazed with boarded-up buildings.

"It's not trout water," I said, "but maybe catfish."

Airbrush nodded. Bucket biology has been a Butte tradition since miners first planted carp in the trout streams a hundred years ago. "No telling what's growing down there," he said.

The Duke had neither heard nor uttered a word. The pinpricks of his pupils were focused on the future with the myopic stare of a man possessed that I have come to both love and fear so well. The look means anything—anything—is possible.

"I have one word for you," he said. "Golf."

I couldn't have been more surprised than if he had said we really were going to fish the Pit. I was sure the Duke had never even played golf. "Golf?" I said. "You're serious?"

"People keep telling me about golf," said the Duke. He drummed his fingers on the steering wheel in time with the Talking Heads on the tape deck. "You have to try it, I keep hearing. So I thought: What better place to learn than Butte in a high wind?"

We swung in a wide curve into the parking lot at the Butte Country Club, which is a combination of oddities akin to a polka band at the coronation of the new Queen of England. Even so, nobody accused us of being overdressed as we walked into the Pro Shop. We all three wore rubber river sandals and Hawaiian shorts. Duke and I had palm-tree and toucan shirts to match, but Airbrush stole the show with a stained T-shirt bearing an outline of the state of Montana surrounding the words "Gut shoot 'em at the border."

A fat man who hadn't shaved in the last couple of days stood behind the counter. He looked us over, then bobbed his three stubbled chins knowingly.

"You must be the missing Kiwanis," he said, pronouncing it "Kye-wanees."

"Sorry we're late." The Duke never missed a beat. He shook the counterman's hand. "Car trouble."

"Yeah," grinned the counterman and introduced himself as Earl, "I figgered it was either that or you had to get the lawn mowed first."

Earl handed us blank name tags, clubs, and the keys to a golf cart. His whiskered grin grew to a smile as Duke explained the concept of D.T.I. to him. Then Earl pointed to a battered green Igloo cooler beside the rack of putters, and added, "Don't forget yer beer. There's more ice if you need it."

"Thanks," we said and meant it. You can never have too much ice.

We had just been invited to join an all day golf scramble and drinking bash hosted by a whole medley of fraternal lodge organizations. Elks, Moose, and Eagles strolled about the first tee. Most of the people were meeting for the first time; our identities seemed secure, but since you can't be too careful we traded our fishing hats for the fezzes of three staggering-drunk Shriners from Anaconda, then filled out our name cards as Methyl, Ethyl, and Nitrate Blitz.

Not all of the Blitz Brothers were strangers to a golf course. One of them had even played in college. Ethyl had the distance, Methyl the hot irons, and Nitrate, to his bemused delight, found that he could putt. Just like lining up the eight ball for a bank shot, he said. The Brothers for as long as they could maintain their momentum atop the bell curve of enhanced perception were like besotted Jedi knights: the force was with them. The tournament was a scramble, a format ideally suited to their condition.

On the holes that ran with the wind the Brothers were absolutely splendid. They birdied the first and third, then Nitrate drained a thirty-foot putt for eagle from the fringe on the par five sixth. First prize was two hundred dollars, and the Blitz Brothers had already decided to spend it all in one place—like maybe Idaho. Then, on the eighth, Methyl was driving the cart in the rough searching for a hooked ball and lighting a cigar when he should have been watching where he was going. All three brothers hiked the tall weeds to the car, then stopped at a drug store, bought a postcard, drew a map to the cart and signed it with a sketch of a scuba diver, then continued fishing toward the Big Hole River, where it was deemed by popular acclaim to be cocktail hour, and time to switch to gin.

We were out of gin; fortunately the Blue Moon Saloon was rising at the edge of the road through the front windshield. The Blue Moon is both a fisherman's bar on the Big Hole River, and one of those "last chance for gas" outposts on a lonely stretch of an interstate highway running from the Mexican desert to the Canadian plains. The Blue Moon is also home to Montana's most crotchety bartender, which is saying something.

"Got any gin?" I asked when we walked in.

"Course we got gin," said Lois. Her tone made snide seem insipid.

"Great," I said. "Gin and tonic. Double lime."

"Two," said Airbrush holding up thumb and index finger, "in a tall glass."

"Bombay Martini," said Duke, "Hold the vermouth, double olive. And a pack of Marlboros."

Lois spun on her heel. She muttered something under her breath about "demanding yuppie shithead pricks," then jerked up a clear plastic bottle and waved it in our faces like a club.

"I said we got gin and we do and this is it and if you don't like it," she said, pausing for breath, then finishing, "you can get the sweet hell out of here and find your own damn gin."

The Duke got down on one knee and looked up at Lois. "Will you marry me?" he asked.

Lois looked over the six and a half feet of muscle that is the Duke and said, "You ain't near man enough for me." She then poured the drinks, folded her arms across her drooping breasts, and stared out the window. That's the way Lois is, and once you get past the insults she's just a lonely lady who can make you laugh if she wants to.

A worn universal joint clanked as a battered white one-ton step van rolled to a stop at the single gas pump (regular) out front. Orange county license plates. Long rolls of frayed green astro turf were strapped to the van sides; wire cages that reminded me of lobster traps were perched precariously in a mound on the roof. The driver was California beautiful, all curving tan skin and gleaming white teeth as she climbed from the cab.

The woman read the "Pay First" sign on the locked pump and came inside. She leaned next to me on the counter so close I caught a salty whiff of her long hot day on the road. The girl absently wiped a wandering golden blonde bang back into place on her forehead.

"Twenty dollars worth of gas," she said, "and a mineral water. With a glass of ice."

I waited for Lois to explode, and wasn't disappointed. Mineral water and the people who drink it are two of her favorite topics. The California girl turned to me as if for an explanation of the outburst. I shrugged.

"Have a beer," I said. "This is Montana."

"A beer?" she replied.

"You say you want a beer?" Lois cupped her hand to her ear and looked at the girl.

"I don't know." The girl paused to consider.

"You want a beer or not?" Lois rapped the bar with her fist. "Make up your mind now."

"Go ahead," I said. "I'm buying."

"Sure," said the girl to Lois, "He's buying," then she turned to look at me.

"What does being in Montana have to do with drinking beer?" she asked.

"Out here in the boondocks," I replied, "we're a good fifteen years behind the rest of the country. We don't have a lot of high culture, but we don't have gang wars either. We'll get white wine and mineral water about the time man walks on Mars."

"And you," she replied, tapping my name tag with her forefinger, "must be Ethyl."

"Oh that," and then the Blitz Brothers told the story of their abbreviated golf career in three part harmony with sound effects, and fezzes from the back seat, and circles and arrows drawn with black Keno crayons on the back of bar napkins, until even Lois laughed.

The blonde introduced herself as Peggy. She liked to talk. She sipped her beer, said she was lucky and had high metabolism and never had to watch her weight, then said she was a struggling actress from the Midwest who had moved to Hollywood. So far there had been a few commercials and some bit parts in the soaps, but in southern California, she finished, actress was just another word for unemployed.

"It's the same with river guides in Montana," I agreed. "It snows ten months a year."

I tried to think of what to say next.

"So what's with all the carpet and cages hanging off your van?" I asked. "Props for a play that you're in?"

"I wish," she said. "Acting doesn't pay the bills, so I show dogs."

"You mean like poodles and schnauzers and pedigrees? In a ring with judges?"

Peggy held her cold bottle of beer up to her temple, sighed, and said, "Exactly."

"And you get paid for this?"

"More than you'd think. I'm on my way now to Calgary for a big show."

Peggy looked at her watch, said it had been fun but she had to go. I said it was nice to meet you and watched her walk away. Too bad. We had laughed well together. Peggy stopped and made a call from the pay phone outside, then hung the receiver up a trifle too hard. She lifted her face to the heavens and shook her arms at the sky, then returned to the bar.

"Back so soon?" I said.

"You say you're an out-of-work river guide?" she replied getting straight to the point.

"Just until next Wednesday." I pushed a ten across the bar and bought another round. "Then it's eight days straight."

"Well," she said, "I could use some help. I just found out I'm picking up six more dogs at the show. It's more than I can really handle. Do you know anything about dogs?"

"Just that they bite at one end," I said, "and stink at the other."

"That's enough." Head up, shoulders back, Peggy was all business. "I can pay fifty a day and food. All you'll have to do is walk and feed the dogs. Take you maybe four hours every afternoon."

Well, that didn't sound too bad. The Bow River flows through downtown Calgary, and afternoons are usually the worst time to fish anyway.

But, despite the sybaritic pleasures inherent in these short-term relationships, the reality of life without commitment was mostly loneliness. I felt more strongly with each passing year as if I were missing something, something critical to that state of being known as happiness, until one August at a music festival on the Dearborn River.

This festival is a camp-out sponsored by an eccentric group of musicians called the Greater Helena Parlour Pickin' Society, and features a musical amalgam of everything from rock to swing, dedicated at the core to some of the smoothest, cleanest old-time fiddle music anywhere. Day and night the fields of yellow mountain clover are sprinkled with knots of T-shirted troubadours roving from group to group with the randomness of excited musical electrons jumping between energy levels. It's a four-day party, and sleep is optional: if you ever heard an accordion and a bagpipe laying into "Dueling Banjos" at three in the morning you would know why.

It's a long weekend, and time enough to see old friends. It's also a time to meet new ones, and in one of those years there was a new girl in town. Maybe a lawyer. Hard to tell. The sticker on her guitar case said: "Real Musicians Have Day Jobs."

She was just up from New Orleans, and sang the old gospel songs in a voice that stayed sweet through even the highest of glass-breaking notes. She was buxom and charming, so smart it was disconcerting, a world-class flirt, and constantly surrounded by guys vying for her attention. After three days I hadn't even yet spoken with the girl (although she had glared at me several times when I was in search of the lost chord) when after breakfast she surprised me by grabbing lightly at my elbow as I walked by on my way to wet-wade the river.

"I'm Patsy," she said, then pointed and asked, "And what's that?"

I looked down. She was pointing at my crotch. I looked back at her face and she smiled. I tried to come up with something clever to say, but I couldn't concentrate.

"Is that a fly rod," she drawled, changing her point slightly now that she had me off balance where she wanted me. Patsy then said she had been fishing with her father since she was a kid, that she never, ever tired of fishing, and that she had never been fly-fishing.

"Nevah, Evah," she repeated into the silence as she waited for me to get the hint.

"Never?" I replied, then gathered my wits and added, "Would you like to try it?"

Patsy said yes, that would be nice, and went to change into her bathing suit.

I thought it was my lucky day, but I discovered later it wasn't as spontaneous as all that. Patsy, now that she lived in the mountains, really did want to try fly-fishing. She didn't have any gear; I was fingered through the grapevine as a fly-fishing guide most likely to have good equipment. The rest was easy for a girl like Patsy with a guy like me.

I didn't mind though.

For one thing, there was her white bikini. For another, there wasn't much of it.

Patsy was one of those people who did everything well. She was a natural athlete who had gone to college on a basketball scholarship, and within the first twenty minutes of instruction she was casting half the fly line. Her loops furled and unfurled front and back against the dark red cliff walls of the river canyon. It's a sight I'll never forget. The piercing cry of a red-tailed hawk echoed down. I don't think I would ever get tired of this, she said, and I said I knew I wouldn't.

Before long Patsy landed her first trout—an eight-inch brown. She giggled with delight; by way of thanks, later that night, in the wee hours, by the light of the coming moon, she kissed me with her tongue. We had been carrying on playing music and passing the whisky bottle; I had just asked Patsy into my tent.

She declined and said: "Not on the first date. I'm an old-fashioned girl." Then Patsy kissed me again. I told her she wasn't that old-fashioned. "Not tonight," she repeated, then smiled and said, "But I'd like it if you came over for dinner next Tuesday. About six."

Hey-hey, I was thinking. Zippity-doo-dah. She likes me! Fishing and music. And she was so beautiful. Talk about shared passion. How could this relationship miss? It was a match made in heaven. Or was it? Dinner was not the intimate candlelit affair I had expected. There was already a crowd of people present when I arrived. I had been trying for relaxed and confident; I settled for holding my shoulders forward to cover the wet spots under my arms as Patsy walked up.

"You smell so nice," she said and buried me in a soft hug. Then she looked up, and waved her arm to take in the crowd of people. "I hope you don't mind—I told you I'm an old-fashioned girl. This is part of who I am."

I couldn't have been more surprised than if I had been electroshocked.

It was a weekly meeting of the "Way Ministry."

There I suddenly was: surrounded by an encroaching ring of born-again Christians with an emphasis on New Testament evangelism. Custer had a better chance of escaping than I did, and as the circle of smiles closed in around me, I told myself to be careful. I was falling in love like never before, but I was playing with fire. Patsy knew every trick in the book, and all she wanted was what she wanted. I'd been had. Again.

We all played volleyball, grilled burgers and chicken, and washed down dinner with hearty red wine. The people were friendly, the conversations stimulating. It was all deceptively normal until after dinner, when everyone sat in a big circle holding hands. It was touchy-feely time. Each person in turn spilled out their problems, which had mainly to do with the difficulty a practicing Christian had interacting with a pagan workday world, and by the time they had gone around the circle half the room was in tears. Everyone forgave everyone else, everyone hugged everyone else, then it was time for a Bible reading.

They asked me to do the honors. I surprised them by accepting.

I gazed about the circle of smiling faces, and saw everywhere rosy cheeks flushed with the rapture of God. I felt the power, and realized how it was that bizarre religious cults could flourish in this crazy modern world where so many people search for some kind of meaning in their existence. I remembered for the first time in a long time all those many years I spent in Sunday School, and what a good storyteller my teacher had been, and how much I had enjoyed those hours of Bible stories.

I opened to one of my favorites.

This Bible story opens with Jesus on the shores of the Sea of Galilee. He is surrounded by a hungry multitude of his followers. Jesus has to feed all these people, but he has no food. Things are looking grim. The crowd is becoming an unruly mob. It could be the Donner Party two thousand years ahead of time. We're talking a barbarian barbecue here. Jesus needs a miracle, which is precisely what he gets: Wine, loaves of bread, and fish all begin to fall from the sky. What a day. Soon there is enough food for everyone in the throng to fill their bellies, and, presumably (since Jesus was a fisherman) enough wine to get everybody loaded, although the Bible glosses over this part.

I finished the story with gusto. Everyone was looking at me.

"You're a fisherman," someone said, "What do you think about those verses?"

By now I had imbibed of so much red wine myself that I forgot to be careful even though it was clear nothing good could come of arguing religion with this crowd. I knew that once I stopped talking I would never get another chance to finish; so I took a deep, deep breath and said all in a piece:

"I don't believe in a literal interpretation of the Bible because somebody had to write the book and it's too good a story and somebody stretched the facts which isn't surprising since it's really a fishing story. I said I do think somebody named Jesus probably lived and he may have been a great person but he was certainly a great fisherman because he went out on the lake in his boat and caught enough fish for everybody and shared them with a hungry crowd of people and his kindness prompted others to share what they had and Jesus's legend as an all-around-nice-guy and good fisherman grew and every night there was wine and bread and fish and I'd like to think a rocking beach party with lutes and lyres and dancing and carrying-on Nazareth-style. I said there is a lesson here but it's not about miracles because it's about sharing and cooperation and working together for the common good."

Well, I finally had to stop for a breath, and you would have thought all those people had just been goosed the way they jumped up together intent on saving my soul. They had no idea what a job they had set upon themselves. They would have had better luck turning lead to gold.

I am devout in my agnosticism.

All I know for sure is that the future is unknown and unknowable, and I know this like a mountain knows its rocks. I see the natural order in the beauty of a sunrise, in the power of a child's smile, in the force of gravity. I see a world of wonder and mystery where although it seems anything is possible, when I look at the scope of human suffering on this crowded planet I find the idea of a benevolent, omnipotent God to be ludicrous.

And that's what I told Patsy one night when she asked me what I thought. It was about a month later; we had been fishing a few more times, played music a few more times, and now we were tangled up in the lemon-scented flannel sheets covering her futon. The slick sweat on her bare chest was drying in the cool breeze of an open window; I marveled aloud that any one person could have two such perfect breasts, but wondered to myself if this relationship could last. We had so many things in common, but religion is a hard one to get past. Patsy sighed and nestled her head on my shoulder.

"You really don't believe in miracles?" she asked.

"If it rained red wine," I said and left it that, "I'm not surprised a fisherman was behind it."

But miracles were something else I was wrong about.

There's no other way to explain the birth of a child. It's the miracle of life.

It was birth that helped me finally understand love — it wasn't until I held a just-born child in my arms that I knew the nature of absolute, unqualified, I'd-be-willing-to-take-a-bullet-for-you love. It was about survival of the species, about the will to live and the driving need to procreate, and is at the very core of what we as people are. This miracle didn't happen to me until a couple of years later; after a courtship based on the theory of confrontational compromise Patsy and I had finally married, and we had just had our first child.

We had tried it my way for a while — living summers in a small log cabin without electricity or running water during the summer while I started an outfitting business in Glacier National Park, spending winters traveling in warmer climates. The uncertainty of seasonal employment had not been an easy adjustment for a career girl like Patsy to make, and now, with a child, we were trying it her way.

We left our cabin in the pines for the city, where Patsy resumed her career. I sold my business, and we bought a house. We now had two children, electricity, running water, a mortgage, and hospital bills. I was working six and even seven days a week building houses. Patsy worked as much as me and more at home. It was the great American dream, but the monotony of regular employment was not an easy adjustment for a trout bum like me to make, and we were so busy that at times I missed the peaceful mountains where the phone didn't ring so much I thought I would burst.

That's when I knew that I had to go fishing. No matter what. I had to stop and smell the river. I had to. It was time to leave it all behind for a day. On one of those days, after I fished, I had stopped at the Craig Bar on the Missouri River for a Polish dog, and I felt like my eyes were bleeding.

"Hot, ain't it?" said Joe the bartender.

Beads of sweat collected like raindrops on my forehead. Hot didn't even begin to describe that mustard. Joe leaned close beneath his bushy grey eyebrows to whisper:

"It's the gin what gives it the kick."

Gin? I had been thinking Drano. I drained my beer in two gulps, and pointed to the squeeze bottle of dark-brown mustard. "What else is in there?" I wheezed.

Joe winked conspiratorially, wiped the counter with a wet rag, glanced about to ensure nobody could overhear his secret recipe, then muttered, "One part Chinese mustard powder, one part gin, a touch of horeseradish, and just enough flat beer so's to make the whole pot-works thin enough to spread and thick enough to stick."

The cold beer had helped, but the mustard fire was still smoking away in my sinus cavities. I pushed my empty mug across the counter for a refill. "Well, whatever's in there," I said, "it doesn't hurt your beer sales any."

Joe grinned; I reached into the pocket of my flannel shirt for my last five bucks. Joe rang up the bill, and I left the change on the bar. At least I wasn't cold anymore. Eating that mustard was like pulling a chair too close to the fire. And my frustration was melting away.

I had been chilled to the bone after wet-wading the evening caddis hatch until after dark in what passes for the heat of a Montana summer. I had been out so late because even though I was already supposed to be back home I couldn't bring myself to quit fishing: at the time, the sparkle caddis pupa was a recent fly-tying innovation to which the trout had not yet grown wary, and that evening fish after fish had savaged the fly during a constantly mended down-and-across swing.

Still, it had been a frustrating evening of fishing.

I had broken off every one of those fish on the strike—the trout struck so hard on a tight line that fly after fly snapped off in mouth after mouth until I was left with an empty fly box. And I didn't know why. I wondered if maybe my rod was too stiff? Wind knots? Or if I should release a loose coil of line with my stripping hand at the strike? What about using thicker tippet? Strike down instead of up? Is there a better way to mend? What the hell was I doing wrong? How could I have broken off two dozen flies?

I wandered away with my thoughts and my Deluxe Polish Dog (sauerkraut and onions), a foil bag of chips, and another beer. After so many hours of standing in the river I plopped gratefully down into a rickety chair at a dark corner table behind the jukebox. A tall man and a thin man sauntered over, and stood flickering in the neon glow of the classic old Wurlitzer as they scrolled through the chrome-bordered pages of the play list.

Tall was fat and Thin was bearded.

I knew the men by sight, but not by name. They both worked on the Fish and Game summer shocking crews. It was their job to inventory the fish in lakes and rivers using electroshock therapy to stun, count, and measure each population. These are guys with the inside scoop on the best fishing and the biggest fish, but they're not supposed to talk about it. It didn't bother me that I was hidden in the shadows, perfectly placed for a little eavesdropping.

"Hank Junior?" Tall leaned down to scratch a mosquito bite on his leg.

"Sure." Thin's voice was high and squeaky. "Reba? We gotta have some Reba."

"Ah'd have as much of that as I could git." Tall spoke Deep South. Another immigrant.

"Oh man, oh man, oh man," giggled Thin.

These were clearly guys who had been out in the woods too long. The first song came on: "There's a Tear in My Beer." Tall and Thin chatted as they finished their selections. Seven for a dollar. They argued about Chuck Berry yes-or-no for a while. Finally they got down to shop talk and I put my ears on full alert when Tall drawled to Thin:

"Didn't I hear you was on the Thunder Lake crew?"

"That's right I was." Thin nodded his head twice with every word.

"Zap any big ones?" said Tall, pronouncing it "bigguns."

Then it was back to the jukebox. Tall rapped the thick glass cover with his knuckles and added, "What do y'all hear about this here Lyle Lovett?"

"Let's try it," squeaked Thin, "I hear he has a hot band."

Then Thin leaned in close to Tall, and like Joe revealing his secret mustard recipe, Thin whispered, "Don't spread this around."

"On my muthah's grave," said Tall.

Thin flashed the five fingers of his right hand twice, then held up four more and said: "Fourteen pounds."

Tall whistled, then they returned to stools at the bar. Loretta Lynn belted out "D-I-V-O-R-C-E." Poor little Joey. I sat and ruminated. I knew enough about Thunder Lake to know it held big golden trout. I needed a plan. My D.T.I. needed some work, and at fourteen pounds, that fish wasn't just big—it was a world record.

I thought to kill two birds with one stone. After nearly three years of marriage I approached Patsy with a dozen red roses and the idea of taking the honeymoon we never had. Let's go backpacking, I said, just the two of us. Into Thunder Lake. It would be the largest golden trout ever caught. And we would be alone. There would be plenty of time to talk. We could get back to why we had fallen in love in the first place.

Patsy thought that was a fine idea. Talking was something she wanted to do a lot more of. She even thought we should buy a bigger tent for when the kids got bigger. There's that common interest thing again. We found a baby-sitter, and drove on the Fourth of July weekend to the Thunder Lake trailhead. After that almost nothing went the way it was planned, although I did catch a fourteen-pound trout.

We car camped the first night beside a large glacial lake in the foothills of the Beartooth Mountains. It was too sticky hot for good sleep but just right for a honeymoon during most of the night, but finally we slept, then, at first light, a cold front descended.

It was the cold that woke me. That, and the fact that we were nestled hip-to-hip in our zip-together sleeping bags with our lower legs in two inches of water.

I peered in disbelief (it was supposed to be sunny!) through the door of our new tent at the dull grey sky. Sloppy wet snowflakes dropped like buttermilk biscuits on top of the four inches of snow already on the ground. We wiggled toward the part of the tent that wasn't under water.

"So much for the weather forecast," I said to change the subject.

"I thought you said you seam-sealed the new tent," said Patsy, not to be deterred.

"I did." I sighed, rolled over, and turned to face the music. "Or at least I was. Then the baby started crying. Then I tried it again, but the fumes got to me. Then it was time to eat. Then it was time to pack. Then it was time to go. I just never finished."

"That's O.K." she said in the too-calm voice of an organized person grown weary of nincompoopery, "but why on earth did you bring along a tent that leaks? We have lots of tents that are already seam-sealed."

It was irrefutable logic. I could have told her about the weather forecast and that I couldn't wait to try the new tent, but it wouldn't change anything. This time we both sighed together.

We couldn't go backpacking. We'd just have to make the best of things.

"How about a hotel in Red Lodge," we agreed. "And it's Saturday night. We'll find the best meal in town, then a cowboy band with a steel guitar, and we'll jitterbug the night away."

But before we left, I had to at least fish. I had so few opportunities any more. And fish were rising in the storm. Fish if you must, said Patsy as she settled with a book in the warm car. I said to keep the heater going because I wouldn't be long. In full winter regalia and neoprene waders I kicked my belly boat from shore. I disappeared into the quiet fog covering the lake as if into a sodden ball of cotton, where it was quiet. Peaceful. Kind of nice. But also damn cold.

At least the rod guides weren't freezing. It was the Fourth of July, after all.

I tied a #14 Hare's ear nymph on 5× tippet and cast toward a half-dozen small trout rising to midges over a weed bed. The fish were small, not even a foot long. Wet snowflakes hissed as they dissolved on the smudged nylon of my belly boat. I rolled ghostly loops of lime green line through the silence. Then, on only my third cast, the water bulged, and a yellow back with a dorsal fin the size and color of a piece of whole-wheat toast broke the surface. It was the biggest brown trout I had ever seen.

I gently set the hook and the fish broke for deeper water.

I remembered that I had read and promptly forgotten that Fish and Game had planted brown trout in this lake to eat baby cutthroat trout, with the idea in mind that the surviving cutthroat would grow up to be larger, because there would be less competition for the available food. I didn't know about that part of the policy; I did know it had made for at least one tremendous brown trout.

Now I was worried about my tippet.

Consultations with my fishing buddies had convinced me that my break-offs on the Missouri were the result of austerity measures: I had been reusing the previous year's tippet, which is a no-no, because the strong, stretchy polymers in modern tippets can decompose in sunlight and should be purchased new each year. This was my first hook-up with brand new tippet advertised as the strongest of the strong, and forty-five minutes later I would have hawked it on street corners with all the fervor of a television evangelist.

I had just landed a fourteen-pound brown trout on a 5× leader.

The fish was a hook-jawed male, fat and healthy with vibrant red spots, but when I tried to revive him I found that I had played him to exhaustion on the light tippet, and the fish died in my hands. I cleaned the fish for dinner—inside the big brown three small cutthroat trout were lined up head to tail along his digestive tract. The fish nearest the mouth was so fresh as to be almost alive, the next partially digested but still recognizable, the last fish in the row nothing but a skeleton of bone and gristle.

Six years later I felt like that middle fish: Just barely recognizable.

We had changed, Patsy and I. Where once we had been passionate, now we were polite. I couldn't remember the last time we fished together. Or played music together. Or even had much to say at the dinner table.

I had gone away to the mountains to think. I was alone, bushwhacking through dog-hair lodgepole pine and jack-strawed thickets of fallen fir. At eight thousand feet I popped out above timberline, boulder-hopped the last two miles to the lake, and dropped my pack with a groan of relief. After six years of planned trips that fell through for one reason or another I had finally arrived at Thunder Lake, and trout were rising.

I thought a bourbon slush was clearly in order.

A bourbon slush is best made in an old tin cup, preferably with snow from a cornice that will never melt no matter how hot the summer, because the cornice is on the north side of an alpine ridge that looks out over nothing but mountains as far as the eye can see.

It's very important to find the right kind of snow.

Once you find proper snow, scrape the surface free of bugs, then scoop out a heaping white cupful. Add bourbon to taste. If you're not eating well, or if scurvy runs in your family, stir in enough lemonade powder so you won't taste the bugs.

The first slush was so good I had another, then I inflated my belly boat and shoved off, thinking positively about golden trout larger than ten pounds. But, as sometimes happens, I fished for the next six days without taking a golden trout that went even ten ounces.

Thunder Lake was nearly a mile in diameter, and ringed with glacially carved granite walls that plunged vertically both above and below the water's surface. The sheer rock walls had all the structure of a cement trout pond at a roadside Hook-n-Cook, and if the bigger fish were there, I couldn't find them.

I didn't mind in the least. I had the pikas for company. I delighted in the pikas because they were so obviously heel-kicking glad to be alive and in the sun after the long winter. I even named them after characters from Tolkien's *Trilogy of the Rings*, because I think pikas (of all the earthly creatures that I have seen) most resemble hobbits.

Pikas are furry like a rabbit, a bit larger than a mouse, with big round ears. They survive in the harsh climate above timberline, where spring lasts for six weeks and summer never comes, by nonstop harvesting of the highly nutritious mountain grasses for as long as the growing season lasts. The pikas dart constantly about the talus slopes with sheafs of long cut green grass in their mouths, adding to the haystacks in their snug subterranean dens as food against the coming winter, which, judging by the dark clouds overhead, I thought might arrive at any moment.

Another in what had been a more or less continuous series of electrical storms was building up. The lake was a very dangerous place to be, and it worried me. I had to let the pikas know that I cared. "Bilbo," I called out from my belly boat, "You'd better hurry. No time for play, Thorin Oakenshield. Winter's coming."

I knew I was talking with rodents; I wondered if it meant I was to emerge from the mountains one passenger short of a full load. I slurped from the old tin cup that had become my constant companion. I was trolling four flies on a lead core line as deep as possible when, out of nowhere after six days of nothing, I had a tremendous strike and the leader broke.

I knew immediately what had happened. Without stopping to think, I had used a spool of old, weak tippet dredged from the pocket of my belly boat which I hadn't used in two years. It was a supremely stupid thing to do in a lake which might hold a world record fish; my excuse was that I had been obsessing on Patsy's poem.

Actually, I had been forgetting about a lot of little things the last couple of days.

Sometimes my brain latches onto a thought and plays it over and over in an endless loop until it is all I can think about. I don't know if it happens to everyone, but it does to me. I think it is because the chemical produced as one nerve stimulates the next nerve as a thought progresses through the brain lingers in the space between the nerves. The residual chemical trace makes it easier for those same nerves to fire again, and then there is even more of the chemical so the same nerves fire again, and again, and again.

My brain was stuck in one of those loops. Despite nearly a half-gallon of bourbon, a week of fishing, and the sternest of instructions to think about something else—anything else—my brain replayed the scene that was now circling my neurons like pictures on the wheel of a speeding car. The scene started eight days earlier at the front door to my house.

I had been building a fishing lodge out of town, and I had returned home unannounced for more clothes. I unlocked the front door, and scratched my old brown dog between the ears. I climbed the stairs to the bedroom; and there on the oak table next to the bed, addressed to Patsy and decorated with hand-drawn turtledoves, was an ardent love poem I hadn't written.

In a way, I was kind of glad.

I told myself, as lightning flared so close I should have been scared, that it was for the best. I told myself, as I tied new flies on new tippet, that it was time to be true to my nature and get on with my life. I begged myself, as I finished off the whisky, to think of something else.

Fly-Fishing with
Dr. Spock and Mr. Hyde

A T   A G E   two-going-on-three, a toddler can use words such as big and little, even though he or she is still unable to tell by looking which of two objects is larger. Although this makes it difficult to decide which piece of birthday cake to eat, it is a handy attribute in a fisherman. My son Kato caught on his first time fishing.

"Big, big, big," he said of the ten-inch brown trout he had just yanked from the water.

"Don't stick it in your mouth!" I said, reaching out too late. "Yee-e-e-ech."

Kato wiped fish slime from his tongue with the back of his hand; in the process of de-sliming he knocked both fish and pole into the rushing waters of Dog Creek.

Remember now—no bad words, I reminded myself as I jumped into the creek after the rod.

Dog Creek is a mountain spring creek of incised meanders and undercut banks streaming ten feet wide through a grassy meadow just west of the continental divide. It was the first week of June, and the wildflowers—purple shooting stars, red Indian paintbrush, yellow glacier lilies—bloomed in the meadow thick as the hair on a buffalo's back to the ridge tops. The last of the winter snow had just melted out, I had just returned from Mexico, and the creek water was colder than I expected. In fact, the water was so cold as I leaped crotch-deep into Dog Creek that the bad words came in spite of myself.

It had been an interesting day.

Kato was at that age where he insisted on doing everything for himself; we established right off the bat that casting was absolutely out of the question. But, Kato still expected to catch fish—preferably big ones—and we agreed it would be more fun if those fish were caught on flies. We finally stumbled upon a two-part system with roots in what is probably the most effective of all the ways in which fish can be caught: chumming.

First, Kato held the rod over the water and pushed the plastic button on his ninja turtle spinning reel to release line. Second, when so many pigtailed curlicues of thick monofilament had peeled off that he couldn't stand it anymore Kato cranked back line as fast as his pudgy little arm could spin the reel handle.

At the far end of the line were about five grasshoppers and a #14 Royal Wulff. The grasshoppers were the largest we could catch in the meadow; enough of them together live-hooked in a string provided the critical mass necessary to catch the current, pull line from the reel, and carry the fly along for the ride downstream to the fish.

During the jerky drift downstream there would be a few half-hearted strikes; it was during Kato's fast-as-you-can-spin retrieve that foot-long brown trout came from far and near to slash at the five grasshoppers and a fly skittering wildly upstream through the riffles. The grasshoppers were so large the fish sooner or later ripped them free and darted safely away with lunch, but the fish often hooked themselves on the Wulff, and Kato never stopped cranking until the trout bumped to a stop nose tight against the top rod guide and the fly ripped free.

"Trout," I said each time, pointing to the fish with the sore mouth flopping in the grass.

"Bird," he would agree with a smile as I released it, or "Mommy."

Kato was at an age where the brain is taking a quantum leap in its ability to learn language. At eighteen months children know about 20 words; at thirty-six months about 900 words; at forty-eight months over 1,500 words. They learn a couple of new words every day, and as I clambered wet and cold from the creek, the air blue around me, I figured the intensity had been such that Kato must certainly have learned a new word or two. I was right.

"Puta," he said.

It wasn't awful, but it was bad enough, and Kato wasn't done yet. His next word was really, really bad, but still, I have to admit I was a little proud that he already spoke such fluent Spanish. Kato opened his mouth to speak once again. It would be a three-word day and I tried to remember what else I had been yelling.

"Trout," he said, both arms outstretched demanding the immediate return of his rod.

I think of my two sons together as Kato—after the character in the old Pink Panther movies who specialized in bungled ambushes of his boss, Inspector Clouseau.

You remember: Clouseau, fresh from spilling a drink in his lap while trying to impress a femme fatale in a posh lounge, comes back to his hotel room for dry clothes. In a mad dash to return as quickly as possible to the woman, Clouseau whirls about in a flurry of karate chops searching everywhere from under the bed to inside the refrigerator for Kato—the Oriental hit man who may or may not be cleverly concealed and ready to pounce at any moment. Finally, having determined the coast is clear, Clouseau breathes a sigh of relief. He opens the closet door and out springs Kato, who, after enough kung fu slapstick to break everything in sight ends up on the room service cart falling ten floors through an open window into the pool.

Kids are like that.

The thing about taking kids fishing is that you have to make it fun—no matter what. Even if you can't pay the Visa bill, the roof leaks, your dog just died, and you suspect your spouse is having an affair; you still have to make fishing fun or your kids won't want to do it anymore.

And then where would you be?

Take my friend Jerry for instance. He hunts every day of the season. He has at least fifty guns, including a cannon. Jerry hikes and snowmobiles, hunts for arrowheads, pans for gold, and watches the bird migrations. He's an outside kind of guy; but he won't go fishing. And he was born in Montana.

"How come?" I asked. "Seems that a bloodthirsty guy like you would be a natural-born bait fisherman. Didn't you go fishing when you were a kid?"

"Every weekend," replied Jerry. "That was the problem."

"We'd drive through the dark then I'd sit all day in the boat while my Dad fished and drank, then I'd sit in the truck by the tavern while he drank and drank, then I'd mostly just try to cover my head while he drank and whacked me for being such a damned inconvenience."

"Nope," he finished, "Fishing ain't no more my idea of fun than stepping on a rattlesnake."

Loco Lake in the Crazy Mountains is a secret spot on private land. Access is granted to a privileged few (and occasionally their friends) only after prolonged and delicate negotiations with the landowner. The Duke had just disappeared into the landowner's ranch house with a half-gallon of Glenfiddich Scotch and a sealed box of Honduran cigars to begin what would probably become several rounds of sensitive negotiations.

Secret meetings with eccentric zillionaires are no place for three year olds, so I stayed in the car with Kato and Little Duke. The kids were rambunctious, road weary, and eager to spring free of the confining car, with zero tolerance for the mandatory rituals involved in at long last returning to a lake where I had once landed a thirty-inch rainbow trout, a lake so good that it was the brook trout we were really after.

Between the ages of three and four, children learn to differentiate between boys and girls, and put their shoes on the right feet (if they want to). They can carry a tune, and move to its rhythm. They adore silly rhymes. They also have learned how to ride a tricycle without bumping into things, and they know how to push buttons.

Little Duke and Kato appeared to be right on schedule: at least they were squarely pushing all of my buttons. After thumping on each other for a while until they both spilled their juice in each other's laps, they were now holding their teddy bears and singing their own words to the melody of the children's song "Frère Jacques":

Are we there yet?, Are we there yet?
I have to pee, I have to pee;
We can drive Dad crazy, We can drive Dad crazy;
Ding, Dong, Ding; Ding, Dong, Ding.

"Where do you guys get this stuff?" I said, wondering whether pee was a bad word.

They giggled and started another chorus. Now they were pounding out the rhythm in hollow, echoing drumbeats on the roof of the car. I was getting desperate. At this age kids are too young to bribe, and rebel with all of their developing egos against pretty much anything you might ask of them. The one advantage a parent has is that the kids love words, and word games, and still have trouble differentiating between fantasy and reality: in other words, they're suckers for a good story.

"Do you want to hear a story?" I asked.

The boys cast sidelong glances at each other. "Is there kissing?" asked Little Duke.

"No," I lied, "No kissing."

"Yeah!" they screamed in unison, "Yeah!"

"Once upon a time," was all I had to say and, just like that, it was mercifully quiet . . .

"In a magic kingdom not so far away, there was an enchanted lagoon beneath a waterfall that fell from the clouds. All the magic in the kingdom was stored in the enchanted lagoon, and every time the people went for a swim a little bit of all that magic rubbed off on them. In this way the magic kingdom remained a peaceful land where wonderful things happened; and magic did the dishes, took out the garbage, and fed the cat; until one day a giant crocodile appeared in the enchanted lagoon, and ate everyone who came near.

"Whatever shall we do?" cried the people.

The King knew what to do. He sent for his wisest advisers.

"Summon the royal fishermen!" yelled the King, thrusting his scepter up and out.

The King's chamberlain bowed low and scurried off to the stream.

"What shall be done!" yelled the King when the chamberlain returned with the fishermen.

The six wise fishermen huddled their heads together. They looked in their crystal ball, but the picture tube was broken, because now all the magic in the kingdom was beginning to fade away. Even the six wise fishermen didn't know what to do, but they knew somebody who would, so they did what they always did. They went fishing.

"The magic fish," agreed the six wise fishermen, "We have to catch the magic fish."

The magic fish was an all-knowing oracle who lived in Ruby Lake high in the Emerald Mountains. The magic fish had never before been caught; but if anyone could catch the fish, it would be the six wise fishermen. They grabbed their tackle boxes and jumped on their magic carpets. They flew like the wind to Ruby

Lake, where a fountain of rainbows gushed from a cliff of crystal into the lake below. The magic fish was working the surface, porpoising in lazy circles.

"Ah-ha!" cried the fishermen, each with his own idea of how to catch the magic fish.

The first fisherman tried spinner baits, the next trolled cowbells with his magic carpet geared down to low. The third fisherman tried rubber worms, the next Uncle Josh's Pork Rinds. The fifth fisherman tried crank baits, the next "taste-enhanced mini wax worm-shaped grubs."

But nothing would work, and it was as if the magic fish was taunting them as it rolled about leaving concentric circles of dimpled rings on the surface of the lake. The fishermen tried trick after favorite trick until they were mumbling incoherently to themselves as they rooted through their huge tackle boxes for something—anything—that might work.

The King despaired: for if the wisest and best fishermen in the Kingdom couldn't catch the magic fish, then who could? Was this the end? he wondered. Would all the magic go out of the Kingdom? Was there no hope?

It was about this time that a handsome young man (whose name was Righty because he fished with his right hand and everyone else in the kingdom fished with the left) wandered out of the woods. Righty had lived all his life in the clouds above Ruby Lake, and once you got past the fact that he tended to put on airs and holler a little too loudly in Latin, he was a pretty good guy.

"*Ephemerella unicornus*," he hollered, "Now will you put those worms away!"

"Huh?" said the six royal fishermen. "Ephemicornus what the heck-a-saurus did you say?"

"*Ephemerella unicornus*," he hollered again impatiently. "Pale Magic Duns."

Now Righty reached into his shirt with all the pockets and pulled out a fish hook. He had decorated the hook with duck feathers and the fur from a wizard's coat into a reasonable facsimile of an emerging

Pale Magic Dun, which is white as snow and three inches long. He made a rod from a tree big as a telephone pole . . ."

"No way, Dad," interupted Kato.

I looked anxiously toward the ranch house. There was still no sign of the Duke. This was the first time any of us had heard the story, and I wondered how it would end, not to mention what happened next.

"This is my story," I said. "I can tell my story any way I want to."

"But that's too heavy." Kato was emphatic. "Righty couldn't cast a tree."

"He was really strong—everybody was really strong back then. It was because they took baths in the enchanted lagoon every day. Now do you want me to finish or not?"

"Yeah! Yeah!"

"Zounds and Gadzooks," said the King just then, "Righty has hooked the magic fish."

It was on his third cast after the Pale Magic Dun was wet and sinking down into the surface film. The magic fish leaped in great shining arcs and then dove straight for the depths of Ruby Lake. Righty's reel screamed like a siren until all his line disappeared and he had no choice but to take a deep breath and dive into Ruby Lake after the magic fish.

The magic fish was waiting for him at the bottom of the lake.

"Now do I get a wish?" asked Righty, because he had heard that catching a magic fish was a lot like catching a leprechaun.

"If you wish," said the magic fish.

"You bet I do," said Righty.

"That's one," said the magic fish.

"Smart fish," thought Righty, then thought some more very carefully before speaking.

"How many wishes do I get?" he asked.

The magic fish rippled its dorsal fin and grinned. "Just one."

"Hey that isn't fair," interrupted Little Duke.

"Nope," I said. "Life is like that, and the sooner you figure it out, the better off you'll be."

"But without wishes how will Righty get rid of the crocodile?" asked Kato.

"That's right," said Righty. "How am I going to get rid of the evil crocodile?"

"The crocodile is under a strong spell cast by three evil witches," said the magic fish. "Only when the giant crocodile begins to snore will the evil spell will be broken."

"Snore?" Righty looked puzzled. "How do you make a crocodile snore?"

"It's easy. You just rub his belly until he falls asleep."

"Rub his belly! Are you crazy? That crocodile eats everyone who comes near him."

"Then don't go near him. Here you are. . . ." said the magic fish, then wrinkled its nose while slowly blinking its eyes.

On the third blink a poodle fly with neatly trimmed fur in a French cut on a saltwater hook popped out of nowhere. Righty caught on right away: crocodiles like poodles better than kids like candy bars. Righty nodded his head and said thank you.

"It'll take a long cast," he said, "But I'll try."

Then Righty went to the enchanted lagoon and made a mighty cast from the safety of the forest. The poodle fly landed on all four feet just where the waves lapped onto the blue sand beach. A flip of the crocodile's tail and it was over in an instant; Righty set the hook just as the humongous jaws with teeth the size of elephants snapped shut.

Righty fought the crocodile four long days and four long nights. Then, by the light of the full moon, he finally beached the crocodile on the blue sand. The crocodile was now so tired from lactic acid buildup that Righty was able to walk right up and rub the curiously smooth and sensuous belly of the giant crocodile. He had never felt anything quite so soft. The crocodile fell asleep almost immediately; the first snore came only moments later, and the giant beast snapped awake, but it no longer struggled. The crocodile then blinked one big yellow eye at Righty, as much as if to say, "Come with me."

So Righty did. He rode on the crocodile's back as they left the magic kingdom and swam to a strange place. The cliffs along the shore were dark and filthy, and spit grey smoke. The trees were gone; the ground was hard and black. The only sign of life was the hard-shelled animals with bad breath and four round legs that rolled everywhere as far as the eye could see, which wasn't far, because the air was so foul and brown.

This was the land the evil witches had claimed for their own by disguising themselves in three-piece suits as city councilmen. They had approved every proposal for every development that passed their desks (as long as it involved a kickback) until every last inch of land had been clear-cut, burned, and paved. The witchs' campaign coffers were so prodigious that honest politicians with an eye toward rational, long-term growth never stood a chance at being elected. When the last of the wetlands were turned into sugar-cane plantations the evil witches had finally been able to trap the giant crocodile—the last of its kind—and with magic spells forced him off to feed in the magic kingdom, so that some day they might have that also.

But now the tables were turned.

The crocodile lay in wait like a giant redwood, sunk in the foam churned up where the ocean waves crashed onto the beach, until the councilmen came down to the water as they did every night to launder their money. They were kneeling in the waves, washing their hands clean of the whole deal, so absorbed in their task that they never even saw the giant crocodile until it was too late, and they were gobbled up all in one big bite.

A cloud of canary-yellow smoke crackling with electric blue sparks covered the land. The factories and parking lots and malls disappeared—except for the few with independently owned fly shops that sold adequately weighted flies—and the land was once again beautiful. At the same instant there was a puff of silver smoke bright as tarpon scales and the air smelled of ozone and the crocodile turned into a mermaid.

Righty was awestruck; he couldn't believe he had been rubbing her belly.

"You're some fish," he said to the mermaid.

"Thanks for noticing," she replied.

Righty was awestruck; so was I. Never before had I seen the Duke list so far to the south. He had finally lurched through the screen door of the ranch house. He flashed a half-moon grin and a "thumbs-up" from where he paused to get his bearings. The lengthy negotiations had clearly been a success, and I quickly finished up the story . . .

"Righty and the mermaid gazed into each other's eyes. It was love at first sight, and Righty leaned in to kiss the mermaid right on her green lips."

"Green lips!" the boys chorused, then, "You promised—no kissing!"

"And they lived happily ever after."

And it wasn't much after that we were plowing through rye grass as tall as the car to the shores of Loco Lake. Duke and I had a plan. One of us would fish solo from a belly boat; the other would row the kids about the lake in the small metal dinghy that was left at the lake. That way everybody could fish.

I rowed the kids first; Little Duke and Kato were trolling with spinning rods off the back transom. Even though they were both catching fish—huge fish that really were as long as their legs and sometimes came up to their necks—they weren't happy about it. It wasn't enough, and they were complaining at the top of their lungs.

"We want marshmallows," they chanted. "We want marshmallows."

Just then Little Duke almost lost his rod off the back of the boat. He squeezed his hand tight just in time, then held on with both hands as what appeared to be the biggest trout yet ripped ten-foot bursts of thick monofilament from his reel against a drag I had cranked hard shut with a pair of pliers. Little Duke braced the rod six inches from the tip over the wood transom, rod butt buried in his belly, left hand halfway up the rod, and kept reeling until finally the biggest brook trout I had ever seen came to the boat. My hands were shaking as I released the fish, but the boys were nonchalant. They had their minds on other things.

"We want marshmallows. We want marshmallows. We want marshmallows."

"O.K.," I finally sighed.

I pulled out the jar of garlic-flavored marshmallows we bought at the Mini-Mart, and watched in disbelief as they smeared both themselves and their woolly buggers with mushy wads of fluorescent orange goo. Kato turned to Little Duke and punched him. Little Duke punched Kato back, then they both nodded.

"Now this is fishing," they both agreed, and then it was Duke's turn to row.

I kicked away in delicious solitude, looking for rises. The Duke spoke facetiously to the boys, who he figured must be having the time of their lives, as he rowed away into the lake.

"If you're tired of catching these big trout," he said, "we could always throw some rocks."

"You mean we have a choice?" said Kato.

"Yeah. I thought you were making us go fishing," said Little Duke.

"Rocks! Rocks!" they chorused. "Let's throw rocks at the ducks!"

When the time came that I had to teach my kids how to actually cast with fly rods I figured it would be like teaching them anything else, so I went to an expert: a kindergarten teacher.

He wasn't just any old expert either. An ex-marine, his style was a kindergarten cop blend of discipline, creativity, and spellbinding story-telling. He had been teacher of the year so many times there wasn't room above his mantel for any more medals. His success stories with problem children were legion.

"How do you do it?" I asked.

"It's all about discipline," he said. "The important thing is to show them who's the boss."

"And how do you do that?"

"What I do is right off the bat on the first day of class I march the biggest, loudest, meanest kid all alone up to the front of the room. All the other kids go way quiet with big eyes. They need to see what is going to happen so they will know what they can get away with for the rest of the school year. When it's so quiet you can hear pieces of dust clanging together in the sunbeams is when I make sure everybody in that class knows I'm the boss."

"What do you say?" I asked.

"I don't say a thing. I light the kid on fire."

On the outskirts of Helena there is a spring-fed lake that is chock-full of fish. The once lonesome lake was recently developed into a state park; by ten in the morning during the heat of summer the beaches are a madhouse of bikinis, footballs, boom-boxes, and beer hidden in 7-Up cans.

But, early in the morning, the lake is still a peaceful place. My favorite time is just before dawn as the city lights wink out, when the bluegills spawn in June. I'm only ten minutes from home, but as I hang in cool water from the webbing of my belly boat, the breeze rich with dew, all those phone calls I still haven't made seem a million miles away.

One day at the lake as the sun rose, the bluegills hovered above their spawning redds in three feet of water. The redds were bare patches the size of a hubcap scratched into the moss-covered lake bottom. The bluegills defended those patches as if their lives depended on it, which they did in a species sort of way; because packs of opportunistic largemouth bass looking for an egg breakfast constantly circled the redds like Hollywood Indians around a wagon train.

The bass edged closer and closer, finally violating an invisible line marking the bluegill's territory, then a bluegill lashed out and smashed nose-first into the nearest bass. The bass pack would scatter, then reform, and resume circling; I wondered at the force that drove an eight-ounce bluegill to attack a four-pound bass, and I remembered teenage testosterone.

I looked toward the beaches where boys and girls were even now staking out turf in complex spawning rituals of their own.

I wondered which was smarter: a teenaged boy or a bluegill? I decided it depended on the bluegill.

Whenever a bluegill charged after a bass, I would sneak a weighted Hare's Ear nymph behind the bluegill's back into the bottom of the redd. When the bluegill returned, again ready to smash anything that moved, I twitched the fly up off the bottom. With dropped noses and raised tails the fish quivered in place with widened eyes as if they could not imagine the sheer audacity of such a bug; then in a quick burst ripped the fly so hard, that on only four or five feet of tippet, the fish sometimes arced up out of the water like a bright blue yo-yo going around the world.

It was great fun, and before long I had also caught a yellow perch and a largemouth bass on an egg fly. Since there were rainbow trout in the lake, and I was so close, I thought I might as well try for a garden variety of the grand slam; I kicked with a sinking line to the deepest part of the lake. I trolled as furiously as a belly boat allows; the way fishing sometimes is, it was almost too easy, and I had my fourth species of the morning.

I lived in Montana and could catch trout any old time, so I decided to get some more bass. Back in the shallows I cast to the roving packs of bass with a rubber-legged popper, then began counting and watching the birds. At an even one hundred I twitched the fly so that only the legs moved, then counted twenty more before imparting another minuscule twitch, and so on until finally a berserk bass couldn't stand it any more and flashed up in a kamikaze attack from the tree roots. No matter how many times you see it you're still surprised.

The trick is to not yank until the popper completely disappears into the closing white bass mouth. Then it's time to set the hook, watch the fish jump, and let him go. If you have the patience, you will catch a fish every cast.

"Hey, buddy," said a kid who had just appeared from the willows. He had a gold hoop earring and "Megadeth" scribbled on his t-shirt with fake blood. "Whudja let that fish go for?"

"So somebody else could catch him," I said.

"I dunno," he replied. "My dad says anybody lets their fish go is crazy."

I took the opportunity to explain the advantages of catch and release fishing — then climbed back in my belly boat. As I was leaving a girl in sleeveless black denim crawled through the bushes. The girl couldn't have been more than fourteen or so; she kissed the boy, then pulled out a pack of cigarettes, and they lit up in the privacy of the willow thicket.

"Who's that guy?" she said blowing smoke in my direction as I kicked away.

"I dunno," said the boy, "but my dad says he's crazy."

The geologic instant it has taken man to progress from sticks, caves, and raw mammoth meat to napalm, condos, and frozen pizza is but a blip on the screen of passing time. Along with language and brain size, a case can be made that it is the dexterity of the human hand that is fueling the afterburners as mankind hurtles on down the evolutionary superhighway.

This theory holds that manual dexterity — including the ability to make and use tools — is what separates man from the apes: monkeys can eat bananas with one hand and that's about it; nimble human fingers are capable of weaving vines into fishing nets, piecing together automatic weapons to fend off marauding packs of drooling hyenas, and even seemingly impossible acts of digital manipulation such as unclasping those devilish little brassiere hooks.

At any rate, you have only to watch a child pick up two rocks and begin to sharpen one with the other before he throws it through the window to know that the tool-making instinct is ingrained deeply into whatever it is that makes us human. If you give a boy a stick, he'll make a spear; if you give him a rope, he'll tie things up.

"Not the cat!" I cried.

I needn't have worried. The cat was way too quick for Kato, and his screams were of surprise as much as pain as I went for Band-Aids to repair the parallel rows of bleeding furrows in his arm. The repairs completed, Kato settled on tamer game: with three one-hundred-foot ropes and knots the size of cantaloupes he spent an afternoon installing a labyrinth of braided nylon between the back of my truck and the tongue of my drift-boat trailer.

The three ropes snaked through a dozen different piles of re-cycled building materials that were strewn haphazardly about the yard. Each pile of salvaged two-by-fours or beat-up bathtubs was covered with an orange or blue tarp; and later, in the cold wind of a blustery day, the wildly flapping and snapping tarps turned the task of untying the ropes into a game of hide-and-seek, but finally I had everything unsnarled. I leapt into my truck, trying to make up the twenty minutes I was already late.

My driveway is carved into a sidehill, and empties into a busy dirt road on a blind corner at the bottom of a mountain gulch. I skidded to a stop at the bottom of the driveway, then turned to check back over my right shoulder for oncoming traffic; and there at the very top of the steep driveway, like a dog on a leash, my drift boat and trailer had just appeared on the horizon.

"You idiot," I said to myself. "You must have missed a rope."

It was all in the hands of gravity now. The trailer started down the hill, making up with momentum for what it lacked in control, the steel trailer tongue throwing off showers of sparks as it clanged and smashed from one limestone rock to another. The trailer bounced perilously close to the cliff on the downhill edge of the driveway, threatening to roll sideways onto the road below which would surely smash my boat into fiberglass smithereens.

Things hadn't been going so well for me lately; as I waited for my boat to wreck my truck and my truck to wreck my boat, all I could think of was a week ago Monday. It had been the worst day of my life. It was so early the birds were still singing when the pale girl in sheer black see-through underwear opened the door.

When the girl saw me, she smiled; then reached out to squeeze my arm.

I quickly sprang back before she could grab me. "Is your mother here?" I asked.

"I've missed you," she said.

"The money," I said, "I gotta have the money."

She replied by slowly licking up from the knuckle the entire length of her left index finger.

Today her blunt, bitten nails were magenta, and ever since the car wreck five years ago she existed on the far side of crazy. Where once she had been a beautiful young woman—a college student and a dancer—now she was a constant reminder to buckle your seat belt. Skin grafts had taken her good looks, and fried food her dancer's body; as if in compensation her scrambled brains now seemed to route everything through the pleasure centers of her turbocharged libido.

"I like it best when you're on top," she said, now sucking the finger down her throat like a popsicle. Thick whiskers, sprouting from the dime-sized mole in her cheek, glinted in the sun.

"Tomorrow's too late," I said, peering into the gloom of the living room for some sign of life. The furniture was covered in plastic. "Your mother? Where's your mother?"

"I pretend you're on top," she continued, edging closer, backing me off the porch and onto the sidewalk, "when I watch you through the attic windows."

"That's sick," I said. Just the thought of it made me queasy.

I was in this predicament because I once got lost and left life in the trout lane for money in the fast lane. Sometimes I made that money through historic renovations of Victorian houses; for the past three weeks I had been scampering around in baggy shorts on scaffolding at attic window level repairing rotten century-old built-in gutters and four layers of crown molding. I made a mental note to wear underwear more often.

"Your mother," I said. "Where's your mother?"

I finally wormed out the truth in between the girl's brazen advances. A lifetime of smoking had left her mother with chronic emphysema. The girl's mother had suffered an attack during the night, and was now inside an oxygen tent at the hospital. While I could get the money, I couldn't get it today. I left the girl panting at the curb, and went to a loan shark, where I agreed to usury in order to cover payments on my short-term debt.

My next stop of the day was at the courthouse.

On the second floor I sat down in an oak-paneled room with a lawyer, a judge, and my wife Patsy. The judge read some papers, then asked if anybody had anything to say. There's a lot of things you'd like to say, but nothing that will do any good, and the hot, muggy room was quiet until the judge spoke again, and it was my ex-wife Patsy in the room.

I was glad it was over, but still as sad as I had ever been, and I wondered about the kids.

George Orwell was right. You can run but you can't hide. Big Brother—in the computer age—is watching, hot on the paper trail of small-business America, scrutinizing the records, keyboards blazing in a cross-referenced fire of government gigabytes, the biggest brother in all of recorded history demanding compliance with an ever-swelling list of technical minutiae.

My next stop of the day was at the Montana State Insurance Compensation Fund.

The place is worse even than it sounds—a world of nothing but paperwork which I hate mostly because it pays so bad. I was there because I had just received a flock of nasty letters from a variety of government agencies informing me of the error of my bureaucratic ways. I carried a huge sheaf of documentation which I hoped would satisfy everybody's requirements, make me legal (which I thought I had been), and put an end to all the nasty letters and concomitant fines.

"We're sorry," they told me at the office, "but you don't have nearly enough papers. Go home and root through that mess you call a filing system until you find more papers, then come back and give us six hundred dollars. Then you'll be legal."

"Well, hell," I replied. "That sounds fair."

My next stop of the day was at the hole in the ground where my house had been. There, staked to a stool with four rusty nails, was a handwritten note from the loan officer at my bank. If a note could panic, then this one did.

"Where's the house?!!!" said the note. "We need to take a picture!!!" The word 'picture' was underlined three times with red lipstick. The bank had good reason to be nervous. One more truckload and I would have hauled the entire house — and along with it, the bank's collateral — to the dump.

I had to. The house was rotten. I had lost my last house during the drawn out divorce, and this house was my most recent in a long line of fixer-uppers. It was the worst one yet, so badly depreciated that I finally resigned myself to razing the house and starting over from scratch. In the long run, it was the best thing to do.

In the meantime, I was staring my fortieth birthday in the face, living without running water in a leaky tent next to a muddy hole in the ground where my house had been. I had been hoping this would remain my dirty little secret at least until I had a new building framed up to offer as collateral to the bank, but now the cat was out of the bag. It was nearly October; I wondered how much longer it would be before I was living on the sidewalk donating a quart of blood each week for the cash to buy a bottle of muscatel to fend off winter's chill.

My final stop of the day was at the dump.

I teetered off to the local landfill, my three-quarter-ton pickup truck filled to overflowing and groaning on its springs with the last load of what used to be the bank's house. I was on the gravel ramp leading to the scales at the entrance to the landfill when the truck coasted to a stop. The motor was still running, but the truck wouldn't move forward.

"It must be the transmission fluid," I thought. "It's been leaking."

I opened the hood and checked the dipstick. The fluid level was slightly low, but nothing to worry about. I scratched my head, wondering what was wrong; that's when I saw the smoke. I belly-flopped down to peer under the truck. The rear axle had broken; friction had ignited the five years of accumulated oil leaks that coated the entire undercarriage of the truck. The fire burned smoky like old tires; pale orange and yellow fingers of flame flickered against the dual gas tanks.

"Just what I need," I thought. "An explosion."

I stripped off my shirt and rolled under the truck, beating at the flames with the now oil-soaked and burning piece of charred cotton, then scooping up handfuls of dirt onto the fire. By the time the fire was out I felt like I had been shaking hands with a waffle iron. There hadn't been an explosion, but to be honest I wasn't sure anymore if I was glad or not.

That truck never really ran again. It had basically burned to the ground, and I needed another truck now—if not sooner. My options were limited because the truck had to both get good gas mileage and be large enough to haul my kids; I ended up with a brand new compact king-cab truck that was the first new vehicle I had ever owned.

Through the miracle of American credit I put nothing down with one year to pay; in the meantime I had a brand new truck—a beautiful truck so new it still smelled of the factory—a brand spanking new truck that lunged on locked wheels into the county road as my boat and trailer smashed into the tailgate at the bottom of my steep driveway.

The high-pitched crunch of shearing sheet metal echoed through the cab, and my neck whiplashed back as the truck lurched forward. I pumped the brakes and spun the wheel, then gunned the gas in time to skid just barely clear as the tongue of the trailer buried four feet deep like a spear into the hardpacked earth of the road embankment.

I jumped from my truck that was new no longer and dug at the tongue with my bare hands. I had to work fast: the trailer was sideways across the road in the middle of a double blind corner that most people took entirely too fast. A pick-up truck came speeding around the corner. "NO!" I screamed as the driver hit the brakes and fishtailed to a stop no more than six inches from the oarlock on my drift boat. An overweight boy of about eighteen was sitting in the back of the pickup truck.

"Name's Bob," he said, then belched and saluted me with his beer can. "Looks like you're having a bad day. Need any help?"

"No," I said. The sight of the skidding truck bearing down on me had given me such a jolt of adrenaline I could have stood off Superman; I had already freed the boat with one hand, moved it off the road, and explained what had happened.

Bob shook his head sadly. "Kids," he said. "Don't it just make you wanna kill 'em?"

Even though I was visibly shaking with frustration, I had to be honest.

"You can't blame Kato," I said, "I told him he could tie up all those ropes. He had a great time — it was better than an afternoon inside watching television."

"I dunno." Bob drained his beer as he reflected, then threw the empty can into the purple clumps of spotted knapweed alongside the road. "I think I'd kill 'im." Bob waved cheerfully as the truck peeled away with spinning tires kicking up a cloud of dust and stones, then called out with a wide smile, "Otherwise, he might grow up to be like me."

No Secrets

T H E   T I M E came when I was constantly tired, so exhausted, day after day, that it was all I could do to drag myself out of bed each morning after twelve hours of sleep. I ached, from the bone marrow out. I wasn't sure why, so I went to a doctor for the first time in years.

He ran some tests, and said it was all in my head. I had been thinking thyroid, perhaps a worn out liver, maybe bad blood— something physical. "Could the doctor be right?" I wondered. "Am I just feeling sorry for myself?"

Mind or body, it was clear that something was wrong, and I was scared. It had become an all-day chore just to walk down and pick up the mail, and when I finally wheezed to a stop there were two letters. The first was from an old friend.

It was more bad news. A clown was dead. Of AIDS.

The clown was known professionally as Harpo, and like Groucho's brother, he was named after his instrument, which in this case was a two-foot-long screaming orange harmonica that squirted water on the high notes. Harpo and I had met in college, at a small liberal arts institution that evidently was, since in the intervening years we had respectively turned degrees in psychology and geology into careers in clowning and fishing.

"Is there a difference?" I wondered. "Does it matter? Does anything really matter?"

I leaned back against the rotting round lodgepole pine post that held up my mailbox, sniffing at the decay on the spring air, gladly wandering in the afternoon sun back to another sunny day, some twenty years earlier, when I had last seen Harpo. He had been juggling in my living room, on a cold winter's day, in the warmth of the morning sunbeams streaming over the mountains through the south-facing glass.

"The, secret," said Harpo, "is, to, think, equally, of, nothing, and, everything."

"The secret," I replied, watching the bowling pins anxiously, "is to not hit the ceiling."

"Don't, worry." Harpo spoke long and slow in rhythm with the soaring pins, one word for every complete revolution, pausing to wait for the red pin between words. "I'm, a, professional."

"Just barely," I replied.

Harpo had only recently graduated from the Ringling Brothers Clown School, and at that point had only one season in the circus under his clown belt with the secret compartments.

"Remember," I added, "I have a two-hundred-dollar damage deposit on this apartment."

Harpo responded by tossing the pins higher still, until they arced up end over end before dropping back down just millimeters shy of the plaster frescoes on the ceiling. At the time, I lived in a Victorian apartment building constructed in Helena during the gold boom days, when Helena was said to have had more millionaires per capita than any other city in the world, and the intricate details in the buildings constructed during that period still show it.

"It's a good thing I have ten-foot ceilings," I said.

"It doesn't matter. Watch this." Harpo switched from soft and high, to hard and nearly faster than the eye. The pins now rose barely to head height, slapping from hand to hand so quickly that the individual pins blurred into a continuous circle.

"That's pretty good," I admitted. I told Harpo maybe he did have a future in clowning, then poured milk in my coffee. "What else did you learn in clown school?" I asked.

Now Harpo could barely spit words fast enough to keep the rhythm of his pins.

"I learned that you should never play poker with the altitude-impaired."

"The altitude-impaired?" I asked.

"That's right." Harpo stared straight ahead as he talked, his eyes focused on nothing and everything at the same time. "Midgets."

"You call midgets the altitude-impaired?"

"No. That's what the government calls them."

"What do you call them?"

"I call one of them boss."

I scratched my head. "Your boss is a midget?"

"True story. He doesn't even come up to my waist. It's not what I expected back on high school Career Day. His name is Igor."

"Eye-gore? Is that the name his mother gave him?"

"No. He developed a new routine. A Young Frankenstein/ Quasimoto role reversal that ends with a human cannonball. It never fails to bring down the house. It's every clown's dream."

"What's every clown's dream?" I asked.

"To be alone in the spotlight in the center ring under the big top. To be a star."

"Making people laugh."

"Exactly." Harpo punctuated his statement by catching the last of the three pins he had been juggling. He put the pins back in his metal box of clown supplies, then pulled out five soft bean-bags. "Five is a lot harder than three," he said, and put the blank stare back on his face as he began again to juggle.

"What about you?" I asked as the red, white, and blue bags whirled around. "Are you going to be a star?"

"Nope. I'm going to be a full-blown constellation."

"Not like that, you're not," I said, and stooped to pick up a beanbag that had just crashed down into the warren of dust bunnies that lived along the edge of the oak parquet floor. After a few more dropped beanbags the sunbeams sparkled with all the dust that had been stirred up. It was no place at all for a clown with allergies.

Harpo sneezed. "Why don't you buy a vacuum cleaner?"

I shook my head. "Because I'd have to use it."

"You should take out one of those personal ads." Harpo dusted off a beanbag, and started juggling again. "Something like: 'Yoo-hoo. Roommate wanted. Some light housekeeping required. Prefer lead singer from all girl rock band. Please enclose photo of vacuum cleaner.'"

"Sex, rugs, and rock'n'roll."

"Hugs, jugs, and rugs."

Harpo had the rhythm now. The five beanbags whirled up, down, and all around.

"That's great." I applauded. "How do you do that?"

"It's like anything else. You just. . . ?"

What was the secret? I couldn't remember, and then I didn't care. Nothing had changed. I was still leaning up against the rotten pole of my mailbox, and life sucked. In the absurdity of an age when we can walk on the moon but babies still starve, when we can bring the dead back to life but we can't afford health insurance, I just couldn't bring myself to believe that anything mattered anymore.

It was all so sad. Harpo had thrown his last bowling pin. Another war in Africa, and now a couple in Asia too. Doom and gloom. Death and destruction. You can't drink the water. You can't breathe the air. The planet was dying, and I wondered if I was too.

I sighed, and looked at the other letter that had been in my mailbox. No return address. More junk mail. I opened the envelope only because it was something to do. Inside the unmarked envelope was an invitation.

JU-JU TRAVEL

R.I.P.

?

1954–1994

*"He died with his
waders off"*

presents

FOUR MEN AND A FUNERAL

I looked again at the printed invitation on red paper with canary-yellow lettering, and belly laughed for the first time in weeks. I walked to the house, grabbed up the phone, and punched in the number for Ju-Ju Travel. The Duke picked up on the third ring.

"I just got the invitation," I said. "Where's the funeral?"

I could hear the Allman Brothers playing in the background over the Duke's phone as he answered, "Andros Island in the Bahamas."

"Who died?" I paused. "Anybody I know?"

"You used to know him. We all did. But then he disappeared. We're going to Andros to either find him or bury him."

"You never answered my question. Who died?"

"I never answer questions anymore," said the Duke. "I'm practicing up for a run at political office."

"You can make an exception one last time for an old friend. Now, who's dead?"

"I never said anyone died. I said someone disappeared."

"All right then," I sighed. "Who disappeared?"

"O.K. One last time. My final exception. You did. You disappeared. It's your funeral."

"My funeral?" I said. What the hell was he talking about? "I'm not dead."

"Hey." The Duke was emphatic. "You will be if you keep acting like you are now."

He had a point. I had lost the spark that kept me going.

I was stuck on pause in a fast-forward world. I never believed in the concept of a mid-life crisis until I was mired in one, and even then I wasn't sure about the crisis part, because the word crisis implies change. I felt more as if I had bogged down in slow-motion jello, and that nothing I could do or say would ever change anything again. It was more of a mid-life paralysis.

He died with his waders off. I couldn't remember the last time I had been on the water. This was my fishing buddies' way of telling me they were worried about me. It's not everyone who gets to go to their own funeral. The Duke was right: I had to do something before it was too late.

"So let's go fishing," I said. "When do we leave?"

"The first day of the first quarter of the next moon. So we'll get the best tides."

"Who else is going?" I asked.

"Harry Mason and the Professor."

It would be a good crew. The Professor has an I.Q. ten points above genius level, but is so absentminded that on another bone-fishing trip he once tried to hitchhike back to shore from a deserted island and wondered why no cars came by; Harry is a lawyer who knows more dirty jokes than anybody else I ever met. We are all fishing buddies from way back, but this would be our first extended trip with the four of us together.

"And," continued the Duke, "you'd better spend some time at the tying table because with both you and Harry along I'm having dead bolts installed on my fly boxes."

"Stealing is really the sincerest form of flattery," I replied, feeling better already.

And so it was, in the coming of the following moon, that the four of us landed at the Moxie Town airport on South Andros Island. Andros, at one hundred miles long and forty miles wide, is the largest land mass in the 500-mile-long archipelago of Bahamian islands. Much of Andros remains in a state of true wilderness—a relatively unexplored and mostly unsettled tangle of casuarina pine, sharp palmetto shrubs, mahogany forest, and mangrove swamp.

We were met at the edge of the dirt runway by a tall man with weathered skin stretched drumhead-tight over stringy cords of tendon and ropy sinew. His whipcord-thin body glistened black as oiled ebony in the early morning sunshine; in stark contrast, the perfect teeth in his smile were dazzling white as he stepped forward to greet us.

The man had been leaning against a battered Chevy coupe—a car that had once been the golden-yellow of the evening sun, but was now the color of rust. Odd bits of baling wire protruded here and there. None of the hubcaps matched, and along with hibiscus, the sweet scent of freshly sprayed WD-40 hung in the air.

"Sure Car Rentals, LTD; prop. L. H. Bannaster III," was scrawled in faded blue paint on the passenger-side door. The proprietor on the driver's side door was "L. Banster" in green paint, and the cooler in the back seat belonged to "Luhroy Bananster" in black magic marker. As we walked up to the car, Harry (who had handled the connections at this end) stuck out his hand and said, "You must be Leroy."

"De pleasurable be mainly mine." The man who must be Leroy—our outfitter—bowed forward slightly at the waist, his wide smile growing until it was the size of a small banana.

"So, Leroy," said Harry, pointing out the various aliases as we approached the car, "Already I see a Bannaster, a Bananster, and a Banster. How many of you are there anyway?"

"Dey jes be de one you sees." Leroy's eyes gleamed. "My woman Gloria say even dat mos' often be 'bout one too much."

"I figured maybe you had a different girlfriend to go with every name."

"More likelihood a man with more name den paint decide to shortenize."

Harry set his bag down on the cracked asphalt beside the car. "And not a man with something to hide?"

"Dat coul' be. Mos' mens got tings in dem closets—but here it don' matter. In de Bahamas I jes be Leroy of South Andros." Leroy pointed his right forefinger at his heart. "Dat be 'nough informationals to find dis man of de islands."

We stuffed our gear in the car trunk. Leroy lashed the trunk door shut with a frayed bungee cord, pumped some air into the left rear tire with a squeaking bicycle pump, and then threw open the lid to the cooler in the backseat. "Some chilled relaxification for you fine gennlemens dis early mornin'?" he asked.

I plunged a trembling hand into the iced Kalik—the self-proclaimed beer of the Bahamas. Binge drinking is a classic symptom of mid-life paralysis; I didn't just want a beer, I needed it. I was terribly hung over. Rather than get a hotel room for the six-hour layover we had between flights the previous night, I had spent the entire time gambling and carousing in downtown Nassau, where the nightlife never stops because the casinos don't close.

Neither did the doors. We were crammed into the flagship of
the Sure Car Rental fleet, holding tight to the Naugahyde seats
so we wouldn't fall out, bouncing British-style down the wrong
side of a narrow lane. Flowers, palm trees, and the pastel pink, green,
and purple stucco of concrete-block houses flickered past in the heat
waves. A beautiful wooden schooner sailed past on the bay.

Harry pointed out the window at the boat. "Are there any good
boat builders still left on the islands?" he asked.

"Why sure," replied Leroy. "I isn't dead yet."

Leroy told us he was seventy-three years old, and had been
building and sailing boats around the islands since before any of us
were even born. It was generally acknowledged that he knew the
waters around Andros as well as anyone; a book about Leroy's sailing exploits had even been published twenty-five years earlier. It
sounded good to me: there is no substitute for experience in a guide.

It was so sticky hot a T-shirt was too much. I opened another
beer, and for the first time, I felt like we had made it. Phew. No
more airports. So far, so good; but now it was question-and-answer
time. We were relying perhaps too heavily on good ju-ju to bring
this trip together. Harry, riding shotgun, turned to Leroy and came
right to the point.

"Where are we going?" asked Harry. "And how are we getting
there?"

It wasn't that we hadn't tried to make travel arrangements. Leroy
and Harry had been working the phone for the past month, attempting to firm up the details of our trip. Except, the Third World
being what it is, almost nothing had been finalized. Not even the
price. Or where we were going. Or how we would get there. All
we knew for sure was that we were going fishing.

We had a general plan—to live on a mother ship of some kind
for the next week, fishing the otherwise inaccessible bights and
cays of South Andros for bonefish and tarpon from two smaller
flats skiffs, but, Ju-Ju Travel being what it is, there were still a few
details that needed ironing out.

"Like the boat?" continued Harry. "Did you finally get one?"

The last we had heard, Leroy was still looking around, but he thought he could borrow his cousin's cabin cruiser from over in New Providence that slept nine people comfortably, and came complete with an ice maker.

"Oh yah mon." Leroy nodded. "Nice good boat. Sof' bed. Tings be fine."

"Did you get the skiffs?" pressed Harry.

"De skiffs, de big boat, de crews, de foods, it be all dere. Tings be fine."

Harry turned to the three of us in the back seat, and said, "Don't you just love it when a plan comes together?"

"I'll believe it when I see it," replied the Duke. He had traveled with Harry before.

Harry turned back to Leroy, and asked, "What about the other guides? Who else did you get?"

Leroy stopped humming long enough to say, "Dere be Gregory, de skipper wid de big boat, and den my son Leeston."

"Liston?"

"Right. Leeston."

"Did you get the diesel?" We had sent in a big deposit so they could buy gas.

"Oh, yah mon. Tank full top off."

I quit listening and took a nap soon after I heard 'big boat.' I liked the sound of that. It seemed safer. I liked it even more a half hour later when we pulled up to the dock and I saw our ship for the first time. It was spectacular—a sleek cabin cruiser, all teak and chrome. A pair of flats skiffs complete with poling platforms were tied off at the stern.

"Way to go!" I said. It was an absolutely outstanding ship. Ju-Ju Travel had really outdone itself this time. This was far and away the best deal yet. I started up the sparkling ladder.

"Hey, you stinking cretin." A man leaned out the window of the bridge and pointed an accusing finger at me. "Get the hell down off my boat."

A thick black arm reached up to guide me off the ladder. The soft voice behind the arm said, "Dat not you boat mon."

"It's not?" We all looked around. "Where is it then?"

The stocky black man looked decidedly uncomfortable. He introduced himself as Leroy's son Leeston, and pointed down into the dark shadow of the luxury liner at a dilapidated old fishing boat shrouded in a blue cloud of diesel smoke.

"It ain't de Love Boat," he said nervously.

Leeston had good reason to be worried. He had no idea what to expect: his roll-out-the-red-carpet view of vacationing Americans had been honed from years of soaking up satellite re-broadcasts of "Fantasy Island" and "The Love Boat." He didn't see how this combination of beat-up old boat and fat-cat Americans could possibly work out.

Leeston, as he looked us over, wondered what we ate. And if we got seasick. And if we drove fancy cars. And if we could fish. And what on earth was in all those bags we had brought along. And why we had to be so big—the four of us together with bags weigh well over half a ton. And, most of all, Leeston wondered how he was going to shoehorn all that luggage and sunburned white meat into that tiny boat.

It wasn't easy, but he did it. When we were all aboard, there was just room enough for one person to move at a time, provided someone was perched on the freezer. The boat measured a meager twenty-eight feet from stem to stern, with a covered bow, a broken radio, and an open flying bridge. A heavy blue nylon tarp was stretched semi-taut over metal ribs to provide shade for the back of the boat. The blue-hued shade under the tarp (a space about the size of a compact car) would be our sole sanctuary from the blazing tropical sun. The shaded area was also the kitchen, engine room, and main storage compartment.

In the center of the shade a rectangular plywood box covered the throbbing engine. Brown grocery bags lined the narrow aisles around the engine cover, along with two fifty-gallon drums of fresh water, a solar shower, a chipped white enamel wash basin, a wire cage filled with slightly fermented live conchs, some foam pads, a spare outboard motor, all that luggage, and a pile of freshly laundered Mickey Mouse sheets.

Despite all that there was, there was one thing there wasn't, and a week is a long time to go without.

"The bathroom?" asked the Professor, who is the most fastidious among us. "What do you do out there in the ocean?"

From his expression, Leeston had clearly been dreading this question.

"One way be jump down in de water."

Then Leeston grinned. At least it was finally out in the open. This guiding might be fun.

"Wid de sharkses," he added, flinging his arms wide to show their huge size.

"Sharks?" I said. "What kind of sharks?"

"All kinds of big hungry sharkses." Leeston smiled wider in reply. "Or coul' be you jus' do like natural-born Bahamian fisherman."

Leeston swung onto the gunwale. He grabbed a metal pole in the framework supporting the tarp, and hung butt first overboard, bass ackwards in the classic pose of posterior evacuation for all the world to see. His grin, as he hung there, had grown a bit more uncertain.

He looked at us; we looked at each other. The single-minded fishing amoeba that we together become on extended trips assembled in the rear of the boat, next to the heavy wire cage of pink conch and green seaweed, and the meeting came to order.

"Sounds good to me," said the Duke, raising his beer in a toast.

"Sharks," I said, returning the toast. "Why did it have to be sharks. I hate sharks."

Harry rubbed sunscreen on his face and neck, then said, "Just eat a lot of beans and think of it as shark repellent."

"Ju-Ju Travel," said the Duke, "Where you get what you pay for, and not one nickel more."

The Professor still wasn't sure about this. "I would have paid extra for a toilet," he said.

"Let me have some of that sunscreen," I said to Harry, then added, "Rub-a-dub-dub, seven men in a tub."

Harry handed me the plastic bottle, and said, "One thing I

know for sure—there won't be any secrets on this boat by the end of the week."

The Professor looked at Harry and said, "I'm not sure I want to know you that well."

And so it was, in a roaring pall of blue exhaust, that we pulled away from shore in our boat the "Dail y Doubl ," a name I liked for its optimistic tone even if it was missing a few vowels. The Doubl was a craft short on amenities, the simple boat of working commercial fishermen—lobsters (locally known as crawfish) in season; conch, fish, and sponges the rest of the time.

Captain Gregory, up on the open bridge, was steering. Leroy leaned forward in the prow, head up and out, sniffing the wind. Leeston sorted through the chaos of groceries as we motored first through the South Bight—one of a series of brackish channels that cleave ocean to ocean through the jungle interior of Andros Island. The bights are narrow tea-colored passageways choked with dense green walls of foliage. And lily pads. Herons and egrets. Lizards and snakes. Mangrove swamp. Humphrey Bogart. Nazi U-boats. Katherine Hepburn in a Victoria's Secret swimsuit.

You know what I mean. It was the African Queen—only better—because it was real, and we were there. Leeston, wedged in alongside the single wooden shelf and two-burner propane stove that served as the galley, began pounding out chunks of tough white meat with a wooden mallet.

I yelled over the roaring engine, "Can I give you a hand with lunch?"

"No mon." Leeston looked up long enough to shake his head. "Tanks dough."

I pointed to the pile of flattened meat. "What are we having?"

"Conch fritters." Leeston dipped the pieces of shellfish into a corn meal and chili pepper batter, then threw the dripping pieces into a bubbling skillet of boiling oil. At least we were going to eat good. Backcountry gourmet is as much attitude as ingredients, and Leeston had the touch.

"Where did you learn to cook like that?" I asked.

"Jes be pickin' it up on de boats. Always find work for de mens with cookable hands."

"I bet there's a few girls that know a good cook when they see one too."

Leeston's black belly heaved in a heart-felt sigh. "Dey be least one gal tink so, but she not missin' me so much now lately."

Leeston, as he fried the conch, went on to say that he now lived in Nassau with his girlfriend. Leroy had called him with the dates for our trip. Leeston needed the work, his father needed the help, and so Leeston had agreed to be our guide—but there was a problem.

The problem was his girlfriend's birthday. The day our trip left was the day after his girlfriend was to celebrate her thirtieth birthday; she, naturally enough, wanted Leeston in Nassau for the celebration. Leeston knew his girlfriend too well to believe he could leave on the day of her birthday; he also knew that if he hadn't left by her birthday he would be late for our trip.

Leeston said that he knew the longer he stayed, the harder it would become to leave—and he had to leave. His father was counting on him. Besides, he needed the money. His back to the wall, Leeston did the only thing he could do. He lied.

Leeston told his girlfriend that we (the clients) had appeared a week early. He said we were waiting impatiently, that he had to go now if not sooner, and jumped the next flight to Andros. Leeston arrived in Moxie Town in plenty of time to discover that Leroy had lied too: we weren't actually scheduled to arrive until the week after Leeston's girlfriend's birthday.

It's called island time. Local events in the Caribbean mostly just happen when they happen; when punctuality is critical it is common practice to dissemble early arrival dates that allow for the tropical there's-always-tomorrow pace of life. In island time Leeston was right on time, but in real time he had been cooling his heels in Andros for the past two weeks, and his irate girlfriend had already heard the whole story through the inter-island grapevine.

"Don't worry," I said, cupping a flimsy paper plate laden to overflowing with hot fritters and coleslaw, "She's going to miss your cooking so much she'll have to take you back."

After lunch it was midafternoon before a salt breeze finally hinted of the sea; ten minutes later we burst from the jungle into a color I had never before seen in nature. It was nearly the green gleam of cat's eyes or witch's fire, and stretched forever in the shallow water above the white sand of the Great Bahama Bank to the horizon, where that other-worldly green met the blue sky in a taut line thin as spider's silk.

We cruised south, dodging coral heads in five feet of water toward the Curley Cut Cays. Cap'n Gregory opened her up. The roaring diesel engine, which before had been merely loud, was now deafening. Conversation was virtually impossible. I stuffed toilet paper in my ears and stretched out in the only available space—atop the plywood box that served as kitchen table, engine cover, and double bed.

A half-inch of wood, a plastic red-and-white checked table cloth, and a thin foam pad were all that separated me from the pounding, stinking, eight-cylinder engine. I was by now paying such a heavy price for the previous night's escapades that I slept anyway, dreaming of bonefish swimming in the exhaust-ridden air of a busy bus depot, while my cradle was rocked by giant jackhammers.

When I woke—in the late afternoon—it was only because something was wrong. I shook my head groggily. No, not wrong. Just different. My very first girlfriend was gone. I had been plugging quarters in the slot for Magic Fingers at the cheap motel and run out of money. My bed wasn't vibrating. That was it. The motor had quit. I looked around. We were anchored in the lee of a mangrove-covered island.

The Dail y Doubl tossed lightly in the chop. Leeston pulled in the two dinghies that had been trailing on long ropes behind the mother ship. He topped off the gas tanks. Finally—after two days, three thousand miles, six airplanes, three taxis, and a snowcapped hangover the size of Mount Rainier—it was time to go fishing.

Two hours later it was time to go back. Harry and I had been fishing with Leroy. We hadn't caught anything, but that's fishing.

I worried more about the fact it was getting dark, and although we weren't technically lost, Leroy wasn't sure where we were.

"You see dat Gregory boat yet?" he asked. "My eyes dey ain' what dey once was."

"Is that it over there?" said Harry, pointing in the gathering twilight to a black speck against a green island that might have been a boat.

"Looks more like a boat than anything else out here," I agreed.

Leroy beamed, a man without a care in the world, and said, "Dat be mos' desirable."

Leroy held course toward the island; the speck became a dot, then a boat. A small fire burned on the north end of the island. As we drew closer the fire grew larger and larger, now raging seemingly out of control. It didn't bother Leroy in the least.

"What's with that fire?" I finally asked, wondering if the conflagration might be the unexpected aftermath of somebody we knew burning toilet paper. "Maybe someone needs help."

"Oh dat?" Leroy squinted. "Dey jes be fishermens cooking dem dinner."

"A cooking fire?" It didn't seem possible. "It's too big." The fire now blazed orange against fifty yards of horizon. "Way too big."

"Maybe dem be havin' friends over for dinner."

It was an interesting observation, because not so long ago these islands had been populated by cannibals. A fire that size would have had ritual significance. It is said by those who know that the flavor of human flesh resembles pork; the Professor said that perhaps it was an ancestral predilection of the taste buds that explained the hot dogs Leeston pulled from the freezer later that night for the evening meal.

"Nothing else could explain it," continued the Professor. "Hot dogs? Out here?" He waved his arm to take in the vast seafood buffet surrounding us. Although he is by no means a purist, the Professor's dietary considerations tend more toward the kosher end of things as a result of his religious upbringing. He shook his head, and said, "Why don't we just eat fish?"

Harry finished off the last of the Vienna sausages that had been the evening's appetizers, licked the pink grease from his fingers, then wiped his hand on his shorts, and said, "That's a good question. Why don't you go ask Leeston?"

The Professor, having once spent his share of time as a fishing guide on the receiving end of culinary criticism, was deciding whether to complain or eat pig-parts when the Duke called out, "Hey, look!" He pointed to the cut between the two nearest cays, where a skiff was skimming directly toward us. "Visitors."

"Maybe those are the guys who started the fire," I said. "Maybe they need some help."

The dinghy pulled alongside. The two men inside had started the fire, but they didn't need any help. Leroy was right: They had just been cooking dinner. No problem. A lifetime of fishing under the tropical sun had burned the man in the bow blacker than any other human being I had ever seen; the exercise had given him the well-defined, wide-armed, barrel-chested physique of a pearl diver or an Olympic wrestler, with each and every muscle bulging in place.

"Hey Leeston mon," the short, black, mass of muscle called up. "You catch you dinner yet? You wan' me catch you up some crawfish?"

"No mon, dey from stateside." Leeston waved a twelve-pack of Oscar Meyers. The definitely-not-F.D.A.-approved red dye in the hot dogs glowed hot pink in the light of the fluorescent fixture above his head.

"Yah, mon," said the Muscle. "O.K. I sees."

I saw too. The Bahamians guessed filthy rich Americans like us must eat meat two, maybe three times every day. Fresh meat is nearly impossible to obtain in the islands — hot dogs were our host's idea of the red-carpet treatment. The Professor took it upon himself to nip this gustatory myth in the bud. Let's have lobster, he said. I'll be glad to cook them, Leeston replied, but you'll have to buy them. The entire food budget had already been spent on hot dogs.

"How much is a lobster out here in the middle of the ocean?" the Duke asked the Muscle.

The Muscle looked thoughtful, then held up all the fingers on his right hand. "Five dollah—each one."

"Anybody got a twenty?" said Harry, and now that it was settled, he turned up the stereo. (Our vast array of baggage included two small battery-powered speakers, a Walkman, and enough batteries to keep the whole thing booming at maximum volume well into the next century.)

The fishermen roared without running lights off into the gathering darkness. Fifteen minutes later they were back, dripping wet. The Muscle was still a body length away when he leaped from his boat to ours, two pale green crawfish dangling from long antennae in each of his outstretched hands.

His gold molars gleamed in the electric light as he smiled. "Twenty dollah."

"Are those crawfish fresh or frozen?" I asked. "Five bucks apiece, they gotta be fresh."

The Muscle looked stunned. "Dey no freezer way out here."

He didn't get the gringo humor, but then he brightened when he saw the Duke smoking.

"Hey, maybe you got extra cigarettes eh?"

"Here you go." The Duke snapped a hard pack of Marlboros forward from the wrist; three cigarettes popped up filter first.

"Dat crawfish divin' some hard tirsty work," added the Muscle once he had his cigarette burning, eyeing the bottle of gin.

The Professor chipped ice with a rusty Phillips screwdriver into a white styrofoam cup, then filled the cup with Boodles, and threw in an olive. The Muscle drained it in a single gulp, then thrust out the cup for another, "no ice mon, tree olive." He drained that in two gulps, then agreed to call the crawfish dinner even for two more cigarettes, a book of matches, and a crumpled five dollar bill.

I just love striking a good deal.

This was one of those well-struck bargains where both sides thought they got the best of it, but the nature of commerce has not always been so tranquil in the Bahamas. In fact, during most of the five-hundred-year European history in the Americas, the

Bahamians, rather than bartering for gin and cigarettes, were more likely to steal rum and whatever women were handy.

It was in the Bahamas that Columbus first landed in the New World. He encountered the Arawak Indians, a tribe as peaceful as the hammocks which they invented. The Arawaks lived a simple existence; lounging in hammocks, making little Arawaks, fishing, and hiding from their enemies—the cannibalistic and warlike Caribee Indians. With the coming of the white men the Arawaks quickly found there are worse things than being eaten; it took less than thirty years after Columbus first landed for European traders to capture and sell off the entire native population of the islands as slaves.

Relative to the genocide of the indigenous people, nothing much happened in the Bahamas for the next hundred and fifty years. Island soil is thin and rocky, not conducive to farming, so it was wrecking—the setting of lights on stormy nights to lure ships off course and onto the reefs—that became a way of life. Islanders settled into a routine of fishing when they had to, and wrecking when they could, hoping to salvage and sell sufficient booty from the wrecks to buy enough rum to tough it out until the next storm.

With such a well-trained labor pool close at hand, it is no wonder that by the end of the seventeenth century Nassau had become the cutthroat capital of the seven seas. A host of nefarious buccaneers called the Bahamas home, including Edward Teach, better known as Blackbeard, and Calico Jack Rackham, who was perhaps the New World's first equal opportunity employer.

Calico Jack hired a pair of buxom young pirates, Ann Bonney and Mary Read, who are said to have boarded ships stripped to the waist, swinging cutlasses and everything else. It was a diversionary tactic of great worth against men who had been so long at sea they mistook manatees for mermaids; it was a first and final vision of paradise that many a newly conscripted adolescent sailor must have taken to an early grave.

The Royal Navy finally cleaned up the pirate problem, and aside from a few aborted tries at plantation life by disaffected religious groups and displaced southern plantation owners at the end of the American Civil War, wrecking remained the economic mainstay of the Bahamas. Even this traditional source of income dried up when the English embarked on a program of rural renewal, and erected great lighthouses to keep merchant ships on the water and off the reefs.

The Bahamas remained one of the poorest places on the planet until 1929, when the first commercial airline flight landed. Paradise now had a front door, and nearly overnight tourism became the first legal, long-term sustainable industry the Bahamas had ever known.

More to the point, over fifty world fishing records have been set in the Bahamas.

That's where we came in. It was the morning after our crawfish dinner; it was time to go fishing. The Duke and I motored with Leeston across the flats, and Leeston had just become the reigning but uncrowned champion of understatement.

"Dere dey are," he said. "Whole big school."

Even from a hundred yards away I could see the brown patch of fish; never in my wildest dreams had I imagined so many thousands of bonefish could be in one place. Andros was living up to its reputation. Leeston cut the engine and poled silently within casting range. My first cast to the edge of the school was not bad for a first cast, and before the ripples from the splashing fly had even melted away I felt the unmistakable tug of a fish.

It was too soon. I promptly panicked, and yanked the fly from the mouth of the fish.

"Missed him," I muttered. "Damn it."

Another fish struck the fly as I stripped it in. Again I struck too soon.

"Damn it!" I was muttering louder now.

"Slow down," I told myself. "Get it together. Strip strike. Strip strike."

Another fish struck the fly. This time I was ready. Wow. Three strikes in one cast. I was more accustomed to something like three strikes in a day.

"A double," called the Duke. He had a fish on too. "On the first cast!"

Line sizzled off my reel. "Amazing," I said.

Line sizzled off Duke's reel. "Outrageous," he added.

Amazing and outrageous only begins to describe the catching that morning.

Schools of fish literally surrounded us. For the next two hours at least one and usually both of us were into the backing on fish up to four pounds. I caught so many fish I decided to experiment: I would never have a better chance to test my bizarre crop of weird new flies. I was leaning back, resting a little, wondering which doll-eyed burst of creative fly-tying insanity to try first. I watched Duke as I pondered; he double-hauled and perfectly led a school of cruising fish with the top half of his rod.

The tip section of the rod had popped out of the ferrule on the hard forward cast. The fish took the fly anyway. The rod tip was hung up on the leader-to-fly-line nail knot, and left a racing wake behind the fleeing bonefish. The Duke had to land that fish, or he would lose the rod piece.

Ten minutes later, with only the butt-section of his rod to work with, and the fly line tangled in the anchor line, he did manage to land the fish. It was a Pyrrhic victory at best. The fish was fine, but the rod was broken. The female half of the rod ferrule had cracked—probably from the stress of horsing too many bonefish on twelve-pound tippet.

These things tend to bum me out, but the Duke just shrugged. "Everybody should be so lucky as to break a rod on a fish," he said. While the Duke strung up one of our spare rods, Leeston weighed the anchor.

It was time for a change.

Having sated that early trip need to just catch fish, now we wanted some tough fish, with a chance at a big one. We had been fishing over soft, unwadeable marl that sucked like quicksand, but Leeston said the tide was right for a hard sandy-bottomed flat where we could wade, and hunt up cruising and tailing fish. We were on our way, speeding in the boat across a shallow sandbar to beat the falling tide.

Every so often the propeller would ground in the sand, and the motor would kick up, leaving a white and green sandy puff in the boat wake. Around outboard motors—the infernal contraptions of internal malfunction that have stranded me so many times in so many places—I worry like an old mother hen. This seemed to be just begging for trouble.

"Is that a good idea?" I asked. "Bouncing the propeller off the bottom like that?"

"No problems mon," Leeston replied. "We does it all de time."

I hoped he was right, and tried to put the motor out of my mind. It wasn't that hard. What a morning. Twelve doubles! Forty fish! At least!

Then the rising scream of a red-lining motor drowned out the high-speed thunk of aluminum propeller on hard coral hidden in the sand. The pitch of the whining engine was already up four and a half octaves before Leeston punched the kill switch. He tilted up the motor, examined the propeller assembly, and scratched his head.

"What is it?" said the Duke, staring sadly off at the horizon.

"Dis piece here," replied Leeston.

The rubber clutch-like piece that attached the propeller to the drive shaft was ruined. The motor would run, but the propeller slipped uselessly at all but the very slowest of speeds.

"Can you fix it?" I asked.

"We needs maybe wrench or pliers." Leeston nodded. "Dat coul' be fixen it den."

"Do you have any tools?" I asked.

It was a rhetorical question—nobody with a small boat in the tropics ever has any tools. There is a lesson here. I speak now from hindsight to all you ju-ju travelers out there: pack a spark plug socket and a pair of vise-grips along with your Crazy Charlies because sooner or later you're going to need it.

Although we didn't have any tools, at least we hadn't run out of options.

"See dat mens over dere?" Leeston pointed to a sponge fishing boat about a half mile away. "Dey might be havin' dem pliers."

Our maximum forward velocity had slowed to about that of a crawling baby, so we had plenty of time to study the boat as we approached. Two men were on the boat, gathering natural sponges to be sold on the Mediterranean market—where synthetic sponges are still considered to be just not quite good enough.

A man in ragged shorts and T-shirt balanced upright in the bow, hooking sponges, jabbing in six feet of water with a tool like a two-pronged pitch fork on a twelve-foot handle. He in one smooth motion tore free and lifted hooked sponges on long curved tines into the boat. The second man was stringing the sponges on a rope which floated on storm-torn buoys behind their boat.

"You gots a problem dere Leeston?" the man with the hook called out, half an hour of prime fishing time later, when we finally drew near enough for conversation.

Leeston described the problem; the sponge fisherman nodded sagely.

No, he said, he didn't have the part we needed, but wonder of wonders, he had a pair of rusty vise-grips resisting further deterioration from the salt air at the bottom of a coffee can full of machine oil. Rube "Leeston" Goldberg pulled the motor and went to work.

"You gots any heavy wire?" he asked by and by.

"Barracuda leader," replied the Duke, and handed it over.

Leeston by-passed the broken piece by wiring the propeller directly to the end of the drive shaft with a length of the Duke's thirty-pound-test braided steel leader. It looked like it might work, but after a lifetime of lying in the mud under stranded jalopies I rank work on gasoline engines right up there with being beaten by a rubber hose. I didn't even want to watch the repair job—

much less get covered with oil that the fish might smell on my flies—so I watched the sponge fishermen instead.

They were waist deep in the water, vigorously beating their sponges with flat wooden paddles to loosen the dirt. They beat, shook, and rinsed each sponge until it was clean, then went on to the next. The repetative whack of the wooden paddles was as regular as the swinging of a hypnotist's crystal. I half-dozed in the hot sun to the beat; a whack became a crack, and I was startled wide-eyed awake to find my fly rod dangling dangerously close to the boat hulls that had just crashed together following a shift in the wind.

I scrutinized the rod: it appeared to be just fine. I wiggled it: no problem. That was lucky, I thought, and resolved not for the first time to pay more attention to details.

Leeston had reinstalled the motor. It was time for the acid test, and Leeston gradually increased the throttle speed as we drew away from the sponge boat until we were nearly planing. Hallelujah. The repair job worked, but only long enough for us to get our hopes up before the increasing torque of the rapidly spinning propeller sheared the relatively flimsy wire leader.

Leeston's head fell to his chest. "Dat be some discouragin'," he said.

It was time for Plan B. We putt-putted back to the Dail y Doubl for the spare outboard leaning up against the stove so we could play musical motors. This game is similar to musical chairs, except you sit down when the motor quits, and once you sit down you don't know if you're ever going to get to go fishing again.

Leeston removed the first motor, and installed the second. That motor ran only long enough to get us well away from the mother ship before it belched black oily smoke and died in a paroxysm of shudders. We drifted with the tide back to the mother ship. Leeston removed the second motor and tried again to fix the propeller on the first motor. No luck. He tried to repair the carburetor on the second motor. No luck.

For lack of a better idea, Leeston put the first motor with the slipping propeller back on the dinghy. It wasn't fast, but at least it worked in a watching-paint-dry sort of a way; and eventually, after four hot hours made interminable because we were missing the best tides, we were once again fishing.

"Finally," sighed the Duke, to whom not fishing is about as difficult as not breathing.

We were out of the boat, wading a small pancake flat. I crept toward three tailing bonefish. Intent on the big fish to the right, I made my first cast since early morning, but the loop never unrolled on the forward cast. I looked behind me, where my rod was lying in the water. It had snapped off like a twig on my backcast, and I was left holding only the cork handle in the flat afternoon light as the fish fed past.

It's the details that kill you. After all these years, I should have known better.

Foolishly, I left my rod strung together and in the dinghy all that whole long day of musical motors. Damaged sometime during or since our encounter with the sponge boat earlier that morning, the rod splintered when stressed by the applied force of my cast. Oh, well.

What a day. We had twelve doubles, broke two rods and two motors, and we weren't even home yet. Visions of cocktails danced in my head; when the Dail y Doubl finally hove into view, I marveled at how such a battered boat could look so good.

The ocean in its own way is every bit as harsh and dry as the fiercest of deserts. One mistake, and you could die out there. After the misadventures which were to permeate the coming days, the sight of the mother ship at dusk was to me like the same sweet glow of relief a Bedouin must feel upon stumbling onto an oasis in the midst of a howling sandstorm. The Doubl was all the refuge we had.

After we had tied up our dinghy, and carefully stowed our quickly diminishing stock of unbroken rods, we four gringos congregated up top on the bridge with a bowl of ice and a bottle of gin in the sea breeze and moonlight, and as close to privacy as we could get aboard ship.

"So, how'd it go?" asked the Professor.

"Well," I replied, "it was the best bonefishing I ever had."

"But we hardly fished," added the Duke, tapping a Marlboro from his pack.

"You too, huh?" said Harry, reaching over to bum a cigarette.

"It was a yin and yang kind of day," said the Duke, and we told our tale of yinning fish and yanging motors. I ended with Ju-Ju Travel Rule #687 — don't leave your rod in the boat when the guide is changing motors.

The Professor disagreed. "I caught a bonefish while we were changing motors," he said.

Harry and the Professor related their story — they had also suffered a close encounter of the engine kind. While they were drifting with the tide toward Cuba, with Leroy puzzling over a suddenly dead engine, they passed a school of mudding bonefish. The Professor stood up, made a couple of lazy casts with a Clouser minnow, and voilà — he had landed his first ever bonefish.

"It's not exactly how I thought I would lose my virginity," he admitted as he scratched at his shock of unruly white hair. The Professor's hair gets bigger every day on a road trip; it was now up to about the size of frizzy football helmet.

"So, what was wrong with your engine?" I asked.

Harry dripped Vienna sausage juice on the mat of black hair covering his Buddha belly, and said, "Water in the gas tank."

"Water! How'd that get in there?"

"Leroy thinks they siphoned from the bottom of the gas barrel when they filled our tank."

I finished my martini. "How'd you get back?"

"We flagged down some sponge fishermen." Harry paused to light his cigarette. "They sold us some gas."

I ate the olive from the bottom of my glass, then pointed at Harry's cigarette. "I thought you quit smoking," I said.

"I did." Harry dragged deep. "But I started again."

"When?"

"Just now." Harry blew a smoke ring that was quickly snatched away by the sea breeze. "God that's good," he sighed, then blew another smoke ring, stared at the moon for a while, and said, "We have a problem that money can't fix."

Cataracts, Harry went on to say, had claimed the once eagle-like eyes of the old man of the sea. Leroy, for all intents and purposes, was blind. They had been running over the top of schools of bonefish all day long. It was hard to take. "But we didn't know how bad it was," Harry continued as he lit another cigarette, "until tonight. We were pulling up to the Dail y Doubl—the big boat was less than a hundred yards away, and plain as the Goodyear blimp on a clear day. Leroy was staring right at the boat—right at it!—and then he says, 'Now where dat Gregory boat? We should be gettin' close sometime now.'" Harry chewed an ice cube, then finished, "You can't find a twenty-eight foot boat, how you gonna find a bonefish?"

"What we have here," said the Duke, "is a guide without a boat, and a boat without a guide."

"It ain't right," agreed Harry, "but that's the way it is."

"What are we going to do?" said the Professor. "The fishing is too good not to at least try and fish."

"Tomorrow," we decided, "let's keep both boats together."

That sounded good to me. There's safety in numbers. Few feelings are as helpless as the one you get drifting in the open ocean in a small skiff with a broken motor. We each harbored for a moment his own personal vision of catastrophe. Mine involved Cuban gunboats.

Down below, Leeston was just finishing up the chicken and dumplings. We stopped drinking long enough to eat; Leeston worked. After cooking dinner, making tomorrow's lunches, then doing the dishes, Leeston searched high and low through the boat. He finally found a rusty sixteen penny nail, with which he hoped to fix the propeller problem once and for all. It had been a long day for our chief guide and bottle washer: between food, fishing, and motors Leeston had been on the go without so much as a pause since sunrise.

"Don't you ever stop working?" I asked as he slid the nail through the cotter-pin hole.

"My cousin tole me, he say it ain't the work kills a man, it how dat work be done."

The same could be said for the on-board sleeping arrangements.

The least worst bunk was the coffin-sized space atop the chest freezer, because it was a single. Next worst was the coffee-table-sized area above the engine cowling into which two large chicken-greasy fisherman had to squeeze. Then there was the open bow of the boat, where the deck sloped down to edges rimmed with only the slightest hint of a makeshift railing.

To everyone's surprise, Harry Mason volunteered for the open bow.

"You sure about that?" said the Duke. "It looks like a sure bet to fall overboard."

"What do you call a thousand lawyers at the bottom of the ocean?" I said.

Harry hates lawyer jokes. "Same thing you call a thousand carpenters," he said with a trace of belligerence.

"A good start," I finished.

Harry mumbled an obscenity, then edged along the catwalk out to his bed. The Professor, Duke, and I flipped quarters for the single bed atop the freezer; odd man on instead of out.

"Heads," I said.

"Tails," said the Duke.

"Damn." The Professor uncovered last; there was no way he could win. "Tails."

Here is some more hard-won budget travel advice: the Arawaks had it right.

The next time you sleep in an overcrowded fishing boat, pack a hammock. It is an elegant solution to an age-old problem. From Columbus's landfall in the New World until just before World War II, when the U.S. Navy began to phase them out, hammocks were standard issue bedding all across the seven seas. Restless nights make for scary middle-aged faces; the professor upon seeing his early morning reflection said it best:

"Now I know how Koko the Gorilla felt when she got her first mirror."

The Professor's wild hair was now acquiring beehive proportions. "I think that definitely qualifies as a bad hair day," I agreed.

"What, you got a job interview?" said the Duke in his best Brooklyn accent. "What for you got no suit?"

I plugged Ziggy Marley into the tape player, and said "Ouch!" as my shirt collar rubbed against the fiery red patch on my neck I had missed with sunscreen the previous day.

"Is that freezer burn, or sunburn?" asked the Professor, alluding to my bunk last night.

"Anybody seen Harry?" said the Duke, turning up the volume on his air guitar. "Or did he fall off the boat last night?"

"Nope. Here I is." Harry came around the corner and began to dance.

That's what I love best about my fishing buddies: there's no whining allowed. Nobody on that ship was going to allow a few little things like blind guides, no sleep, and broken motors get in the way of a good time. Leroy just grinned at the show. I doubt he'd seen anything quite like it in all his years at sea, and as he lounged in the shade sipping milk, sugar, and hot English tea from a chipped ceramic mug, he said, "Ahhh. Now dis, dis be what I calls relaxable."

Leroy had another word for it a bit later after breakfast when we finally ate the hot dogs.

"Ahhh. Now dis," he said, and shook his head, "Dis be mos' sick-appointing."

Leeston had just taken the latest incarnation of the propeller repair out for a test drive. The nail broke, the engine whined, and Leeston was nothing if not stoic as he drifted once again with the tide back to the mother ship. Rather than another merry-go-round of musical motors, we decided instead to engage in a round of musical people.

There was a string of flats, Leroy said, so close together that we could use one boat to leapfrog pairs of fisherman—and everyone could fish. Duke and I went first. As we neared the first green island, bouncing from swell to swell; the Duke snapped his fingers, and shook his head.

"What's wrong?" I asked.

Duke looked longingly at the dry land. "Got any toilet paper?"

"Yep. Sure do." I held out my hand. "Got any flies?"

"What's the matter?" The Duke handed me one of his three very full fly boxes. "Your brainstorms aren't working?"

He was right. I had filled my boxes with flies that didn't work, and I rifled his box for something in pink, while the Duke told me once again I should be incarcerated for the flies I tie. Nobody has ever accused me of being a purist. I told him I couldn't help it, I just get carried away, and I described how I had been so positive back in Montana that I had come up with the next great breakthrough in bonefish fly design. I handed him some toilet paper, promised that next time I would tie more standard patterns first, and hoped it was true, and then we were there, jumping from the boat.

"Fish up dat way," Leroy called out. He pointed left, then yelled over his shoulder as he roared off to pick up Harry and the Professor, "Meet up in tirty minute on de end of de cay."

If you have ever gone deer hunting, this should ring a bell. It's the same as: "I'll meet you for lunch on the old logging road on the other side of the mountain."

The next time you actually meet up with your hunting partner is a week later at the grocery store. "Hey!" you call out from the frozen vegetables, "what happened to you?"

Your hunting partner then looks up with a jar of hot sauce in his hands. "What do you mean what happened to me?" he says. "What happened to you?"

Which is exactly what happened to me. After Leroy dropped us on the island, the Duke and I split up so we would both have virgin water to fish. He went left, I went right, and we agreed to meet at the far end of the island in a half-hour. I arrived ten minutes late to an empty beach. No Duke, no Leroy, no boat. There was nothing but sand, sea, a very hot sky, and for company—a blue hole.

The blue holes of Andros, a vast system of underwater limestone caves, were made famous by the explorations of Jacques Cousteau. The caves he mapped, complete with gravity-influenced features such as stalactites and stalagmites, could only have been carved out by trickling groundwater above sea level. The depths to which these caverns descend suggest that sea levels—most likely during the Ice Ages, when much of the planet's water supply was frozen—were once lower by a thousand feet or more.

If this is true, as it seems, then sometime in the relatively recent geologic past sea levels have risen dramatically. It is the myth of the great flood, a legend so prevalent in the oral traditions of ancient peoples the world over that it seems reasonable to assume some long-term large-scale flooding has indeed occurred.

On the other hand, some researchers have used this same evidence to conclude that the lost city of Atlantis is submerged off the coast of Andros. Their theorem: since the Great Bahama Bank is the place on Earth where the most land would be gained by a drop in sea level, then that's where Atlantis must have been. Using similar logic, some researchers have concluded that Venutian colonists are living in the Tongue of the Ocean—a deep oceanic trench just north of Andros—since the bottom pressure of ninety-one atmospheres in the trench is equal to the surface pressure on Venus.

And that's not all. The Bahamas anchor the southwest corner of that hotbed of mysterious behavior known as the Bermuda Triangle; therefore, speculate the researchers, either Venutians or Atlantians are behind all these strange and seemingly inexplicable events.

Perhaps sporadic bursts of electromagnetic radiation of unimaginable power from the energy sources of lost or hidden civilizations are the force behind the glowing white clouds. Behind the disappearance in odd circumstances of so many planes, boats, and people. The apparent disruptions of time. The ghost ships. The disrupted and bizarre radio communications, and malfunctioning compasses that date back to Columbus himself.

Is the Bermuda Triangle real? Are there forces simmering away below the surface of our everyday world that conventional wisdom and science can't yet explain?

It seems like it to me, but I haven't known for sure since I was about five years old.

In Ohio near Lake Erie it was May—time to plant the corn. My father on the tractor plowed the ten-acre field. Sometime during the day, his black wallet popped from his hip pocket.

"My paycheck was in there," he said.

"We'll just have to find it," said my grandmother, and organized a search party of all us adults and kids.

The freshly plowed topsoil made perfect camouflage for a black wallet. Ten acres is a lot of camouflage. Besides, the wallet was probably buried. Even a small child with a grape Kool-Aid mustache could see it was hopeless, and it would have been, but for the girl next door.

The girl was about twelve, with thin black hair and skin so pale as to be almost chalky. Her family had just moved north from Tennessee. The girl was at least strange and in retrospect I think perhaps retarded—the latest victim of inbreeding in a long line of backcountry hill people.

The girl slipped from her house with the badly peeling yellow paint, and flowed on skinny mosquito-bitten legs in a bee line through the plowed field. I watched her, and couldn't not follow. The dirt crumbled at the edges of the footprints her bare feet made in the warm soil; I was right there a few minutes later when she dropped to her knees, dug through six inches of turned earth, and pulled out the missing wallet.

"How'd you do that?" I asked, my eyes wide, maybe frightened.

She blinked her violet eyes, then looked at the ground.

"Jesus talks to me," she mumbled. "Sometimes in my dreams."

Was it Jesus? Her parents were kissing cousins who between them had only a dozen teeth, a second-grade education, and a deep, abiding faith that they were among the select few that God had chosen for higher duty. With a background like this the girl next door would of course think it was Jesus whispering in her ear; but maybe it was the Buddha in disguise. Or Zeus, Jahweh, one of the cruel Gods of the Aztecs, or perhaps the omnipotent Corn God of the Anasazi.

Or maybe the girl was some kind of a savant. The rational explanation—that she found the wallet because she had seen it drop —seemed unlikely given the distances involved. Maybe mischievous Venutian colonists were helping her out. Who knows for sure?

Personally, I believe not so much in either Bigfoot or the Pope, as that there are forces in the natural world simmering beneath the veneer of civilization that science hasn't explained. I believe that on some days for some people these forces bubble over into everyday life: the "zone" of the hot three-point-shooter in the NBA, or the guy who always catches more fish because somehow he *knows* something you don't.

I've had the good fortune to savor a few of those moments of absolute clarity—to become one with the universe—but never sustained over so long a period as that day I was stranded on a desert island in the Bahamas. It was all so clear. I read that flat like a book; for the first time, I was thinking like a bonefish.

I followed the rising tide along the subtle network of dendritic channels the fish used as commuter highways to the prime feeding areas—patches of rich grass and coral brimming with scuttling crabs and wriggling shrimp. I was casting well; the bonefish raced each other to take my flies. It sounds perfect, but it wasn't. Of the first five fish I hooked, barracuda ate three.

More than any other day I have experienced, it was an eat-or-be-eaten kind of day. It was the Day of the Carnivores. I have no idea why, but the forces of nature were boiling over in a hard-fought life-and-death struggle beneath the waves.

I gave up on bonefishing as a lost cause.

I switched to wire tippets, green needlefish streamers with mylar tube bodies, and a two-handed fast-as-you-can-go retrieve. I'd be lying if I told you the barracuda fishing was good. It was better than that. The initial spurt of a big barracuda is like a torpedo skipping through the waves, a quick burst every bit as frantic and frenzied as teenage love, and I marveled that I had gone so many years not knowing barracuda fishing could be so much fun.

Then, in keeping with the spirit of the day, I nearly joined the food chain myself.

I had fished back to the blue hole. The deep water of the blue hole was a circle twenty yards in diameter, nearly in the center of a shallow green water channel separating me from the next cay. I decided to swim the channel, to search for bonefish along the other island, but I procrastinated, wondering at the prickly feeling in the back of my neck.

I spent the next fifteen minutes arguing with my inner voice: Go ahead—swim. It's safe. *No way, something's wrong.* It'll be easy. That channel isn't even two hundred feet across. *It's that blue hole.* You've snorkeled in dozens of places like this. *I know.* You're a good swimmer. *It's true.* I now stood in knee-deep water, and had about convinced myself to swim when a huge, dark shadow drifted up out of the blue water.

If I had swum the channel, on that particular day, I have no doubt that shark would have eaten me. One mouthful at a time. I *knew* it.

I moved to shore; the hammerhead at one point swam within twenty feet of me. The tide was now full bore and rushing in; the shark held nose first in the current, nostrils flaring, swinging back and forth, obviously hungry and actively hunting. He was an honest ten feet, maybe more, and no, I didn't try to catch him. I'm not sure about my ju-ju with sharks as it is.

Later, I was out of drinking water, baked and thirsty after six hours under the unrelenting sun on an island without shade, and it was high tide. I knew Leroy would be back, but the way things were going, I knew it might not be today. I walked my island feeling more like Robinson Crusoe all the time, and I spotted a school of very nervous bonefish. They were circling around the perimeter of a shallow tepid bay, in and out of the relative safety of the tangled mangrove roots.

Patience is the name of this game.

It is like fishing for cruising cutthroat trout along the shores of high mountain lakes. I put the sun behind me and walked into calf-deep water along the great circle route scribed by the cruising fish. I laid out a cast, placing the fly on clean sand so I could move it without snagging the bottom. I hunkered low, and waited for the bonefish to return.

When the first few fish in the school were over the patch of sand, I twitched the fly. Fish have been genetically training since the Ordivician period not to let anything get away. Instinct makes the fish pounce first, get suspicious later. If you're careful, even skittish fish will never know you're there. Nothing could be more natural, and few techniques work as well.

A small bonefish of about a pound and a half took the fly and streaked left. The fish had no sooner begun to race than it did an about-face back into the school, three feet of black-tipped shark in hot pursuit. The water frothed and bubbled like a jacuzzi, as the shark and the school of at least a hundred bonefish churned in a tight twenty-foot circle.

The hooked fish darted free of the swirling school, then stopped. The shark was still spinning furiously with the other fish. I took the drag off the reel to give the bonefish as much of a chance as possible. Then the shark, never slowing even one iota at any point, in water so shallow he left a V-shaped wake, somehow *knew* and arrowed out of the circling school toward the hooked bonefish with the unerring instinct of a falcon on a pigeon.

The bonefish then did something the experts say bonefish don't do: it jumped. So did the shark, and when the shark's jaws snapped shut in midair there was only half a bonefish on my line. I jerked the rod involuntarily in a gut reaction like Pavlov's dog; the remaining half a fish on a tight line sailed back at me. The shark splashed down, spun in a quick circle, and knifed toward the bleeding fish chunk which was now lying twelve inches directly below my sucked-up testicles.

This would have been exciting even if it hadn't happened at eye level, fifteen feet away in twelve inches of water. I was still in my crouch; when the shark's jaws snapped shut I could see every tooth, and that's when I screamed. I leaped up to put as much distance between my quivering gonads and the shark as possible. I was dancing from foot to foot in sheer terror while attempting to bludgeon the shark into submission with my eight-weight fly rod, and that's when the shark finally saw me.

At that point, I'm not sure who was more scared, me or the shark. He wriggled through the sand right between my legs, ignoring the bleeding bonefish in water so shallow his back was out of the water. I watched the dark shark against the light sand until he vanished into the deeper water, and there, at the tip of the island, just now pulling up in the skiff, were Leroy, Duke, Harry, and the Professor.

I walked down to where they were beached. Still cooking in a state of advanced adrenaline overload, I held up my half-a-fish. I opened my mouth to speak, but nothing came out.

The Duke nodded. "You too, huh?"

Their story would have to wait a moment. My throat was parched as wind-blown Kalahari camel dung. The beer cooler was in the back, next to the big, green round thing with flippers. I ripped a Kalik from the ice, and drained the top half in two gulps, before I realized what I had seen. I pointed with the bottle. "Is that a turtle?" I asked.

"Yep." The Duke rapped on its shell. "A green turtle."

The Duke and the Professor have both dedicated a good part of their lives to preserving ecosystems in their natural state. I would have thought my odds of winning the lottery were greater than seeing those two with an endangered and protected species in the boat. "What the hell happened?" I asked.

"Dis man," said Leroy, proudly clasping a hand on Duke's shoulder, "jump like natural-born Bahamian fishermen, dat's what happen."

The parts of the story gradually fell into place. Leroy and Duke had left me on the island earlier that morning because I was late and they had to beat a falling tide. They were cruising between flats to pick up Harry and the Professor when the Duke saw a turtle swimming out in the water. He innocently pointed it out to Leroy, who immediately swung the tiller hard over; suddenly they were chasing the turtle at flank speed.

"What are you doing?" demanded the Duke, to whom this was clearly an official act of harassment.

"Dey nothin' 'cept lovin' be good as turtle soup." Leroy smacked his lips and patted his belly. "Firs' we runs him hard, den we jumps him up."

"We?" said the Duke as he grabbed at the gunwale of the bouncing boat. "What's this 'we' shit?"

Leroy waved his hand in dismissal. "No worries, mon. You do fine."

Duke tried another tack. "We can't get that turtle," he said, "It's against the law."

"Dat law be no good for hungry peoples. In de States you got plenty cows to eat, but here, turtle be 'bout de only meat we eats. We gets dis turtle or we no eats. And dat's dat."

The Duke was on the horns of a cultural dilemma: there aren't many green turtles left, but subsistence level fishermen weren't the reason why. And Leroy had been fishing here since before Duke was even born. It was his home, not ours.

"How do you do it?" asked the Duke, stalling for time. "Catch the turtle, I mean."

"You jumps him up."

"Jump? Out of the boat? While it's moving?"

"It be easy," Leroy lied.

Turtle-jumping is like bull-dogging except turtles don't have horns, so there's nothing you can grab onto. The turtle jumper balances in the bow of a speeding boat. The turtle is chased for a mile or two until he is judged properly weary, then, at just the right moment, as the boat careens alongside, the turtle jumper leaps onto the back of the swimming turtle. The trick is to tackle the turtle on the carapace just behind the front flippers, get your feet planted, and flip the turtle, which may be as big as a dinner table, helpless on its back with all four flippers in the air.

"No way." The Duke shook his head. Turtles, ludicrously tiny flippers churning furiously, are surprisingly fast. Duke shoved his arm toward the dark green streak in the blue waves.

"I'm not jumping out of the boat on top of that turtle," he said.

"O.K.," said Leroy as he stood up, "den you steers de boat and I jumps."

The Duke spread his arms wide in resignation. What could he do? He couldn't dissuade Leroy from taking the turtle, and he knew for a fact he didn't want seventy-three-year-old Leroy jumping out of the boat. Besides, the Duke played football — and this turtle jumping looked like it might be fun in a contact-sport kind of way. Depending on the nature of the contact.

"Do they bite?" was the Duke's last question as he prepared to jump.

"No, mon," said Leroy. "Dey never bites."

With this placebo ringing in his ears, the Duke, who ascribes to the do-it-well or don't-do-it-at-all philosophy, came flying out of the boat like it was the last go-round at the National Finals Rodeo. Before the seventy-pound turtle even knew what hit him all four flippers were reaching for the sky. Leroy virtually danced with excitement as he circled back to pick them up.

"Nobody does it de first time dey tries," he cried. "Nobody mon."

I listened to the story, then climbed gingerly into the back of the boat. I took the empty seat next to the turtle, being careful not to step in the mound of green slimy turds the overturned turtle was constantly passing. As soon as I came within range, the turtle stretched out his wrinkled neck and tried to bite me with his pointed, brown beak.

I jerked back my foot. Waves washed over the gunwales as we set out to sea bailing with our hats. Together with the turtle we were four or five hundred pounds over the rated carrying capacity of Leroy's skiff.

All that weight came in handy later that night when we became human ballast.

We were making a moonlight run for spare parts to fix our outboard motor problem once and for all; as you might expect, we ran aground. This time, it was in the big boat, our last bastion of safety, and it seemed we were in at least some danger of sinking once and for all.

"All righ'," smiled Leeston, still cool despite the fact that the Dail y Doubl was grinding on sharp coral at the bottom of every wave trough. "All you large gennelmens to de front of de boat."

In the dark, we had run too close to the shoal that runs south of Andros along the Tongue of the Ocean. With our weight crowded forward it would lift the propellers in the rear of the boat, and we might be able to back out toward deeper water. The weight shift helped, but we were still stuck. We needed to turn around.

Leeston jumped into the one operable skiff. He yanked the starter cord, and revved the engine. Leeston rammed the bow of the mother ship, forcing it around like a tugboat pushing a barge, and the oily seas gleamed like mercury as we slowly worked for deeper water.

The moon was just shy of full—so huge that vampires and werewolves seemed at least possible on that strange eat-or-be-eaten day now gone all grey and silver. Puffy cumulus clouds drifted dark across the moon, creating moonshadows that raced at highway speed across the sea. The kaleidoscope of clouds formed and reformed into fantastic glowing shapes, now a whale, now a unicorn, now a clown.

The clown grew larger as the clouds drifted together until it entirely covered the moon, then said, "Did you ever get that vacuum cleaner?"

"Did you hear that?" I said.

"Hear what?" replied the Duke.

"Over there," I pointed, "in that big cloud over the moon, do you see the face of a clown?"

He looked up. "I guess so. Could be. He has something in his mouth."

"Well, he looks like a guy I went to school with. And he's talking to me."

The Duke said in a soothing voice, "Sure he is."

"And I hear music. Harmonica music."

"Harmonica music from the sky." The Duke started humming an old Beatle's tune, then said, "Maybe that's why they call them harps."

"No. Really. I'm not kidding." I tilted my head to get my ear out of the wind so I could hear better. "I hear music. And that's what it is, what you're humming: 'Norwegian Wood.'"

The Duke peered at me through narrowed eyes, then shrugged. He, too, lives in a world where strange things happen. "That's something anyway," he said matter-of-factly. "Most guys need a Walkman. Look at the bright side: you'll never have to buy batteries again."

Harpo was starting to fade.

"Are you there in my head or there in the sky?" I asked. "Is this some kind of flashback? I'm too old for flashbacks. Are you a ghost or what?"

"You mean you don't know?" Harpo replied. "That's funny. You called me."

Had I? It was true that I had been thinking about Harpo earlier during my lonely day on the island. It was part of the reason I felt better. Harpo had gone early, but he had gone well—with nothing more to guide him than his belief that it was a once-in-a-lifetime trip and you might as well enjoy the ride. Thinking about

Harpo helped me remember things I had forgotten: I felt better because at some point I realized that fly-fishing the wilderness was as good a way as any to spend a life, and better than most. So what if I would remain a pauper, living well below the government-drawn poverty line. At least I'd be happy. The hell with what other people thought.

"Is that why nobody else can hear you?" I asked. "Because I called you?"

"Beats me." Harpo blew a bass riff. "I can hear all of you. Maybe they're tuned to a different station."

"What's it like up there?"

"Well, it's . . ."

Harpo's voice had been fading as the clown's nose became a rhinoceros horn then a shiny flying saucer; this last answer was lost blowing on the wind. When the last vestiges of the clown face in the glowing clouds finally disappeared there was a huge water-spout off the port bow like the squirt from a giant harmonica.

"Did you see that!" everybody else yelled together as the music quit. "It must have been a whale."

"Mus' be," said Leroy. "But dere no whales nowabouts. Not dis time of de year."

True Love

HER FACE was hidden by long dark hair. I was standing on a tropical beach, wearing only a pair of sun-bleached shorts, playing languid waltzes on my fiddle. Tarpon rolled in the bay. Her wet T-shirt was cool against my bare back.

She whispered in my ear. "Don't stop playing."

The tarpon surrounded a school of bait fish as her warm hips swayed through soft circles against my thigh. The water frothed, and the woman tickled the curly hair on my chest with her long, slender fingers. Glass minnows leaped frantic from the sea. Her brown hand finally slid down along my quivering stomach muscles, and lightly circled my ringing bell.

"My ringing bell?" I thought, "I don't have a ringing bell," then I bolted awake. The bed was drenched with sweat. The phone was ringing.

"I've gotta get a girlfriend," I said aloud to the four walls, then looked at the clock, and rolled over to pick up the phone. "It's three A.M.," I said to whoever it was, "and this better be good. You wouldn't believe the dream I was having."

It was Armstrong. "I know it's late," he replied, "I wanted to make sure you were asleep before I called." Then he went on to make me a late night job offer. "A horse rolled over on Big Rick this afternoon. He's in the hospital, and I'm a guide short this week. Any chance you can help me out?"

"It depends," I replied. "What's the deal?"

"Thirty-five, and the grubs on us."

"Thirty-five?" I tried to clear my head. "Thirty five what?"

"A day."

"Thirty-five dollars a day! No way! What kind of sweat shop are you running up there?"

"Plus tips. Usually a Franklin, sometimes a deuce."

"I should have just let the phone ring," I said.

"On the other hand," I thought, "My truck needs tires." The rent was due, I had a hole in my waders, and the price of draft beer was up a quarter. A Ben Franklin or two sweetened the pot, but still, even by the bohemian fish now/pay later standards to which I ascribed, that was lousy money.

"Good food." Armstrong broke the prolonged silence. "We just got a new cook. She's studying up to be a dancer."

"What kind of dancer?" I asked. I was just curious.

"I bet she's a good one. She has those long, long legs like you hardly ever see."

Armstrong was floating a howling wulff attractor pattern in the surface film of my stream of thought. The presentation was perfect. I couldn't help but rise to the offer, even though I knew he was probably lying through the few tobacco-stained teeth he had left.

"Is that right?" I said.

"And she doesn't have a boyfriend, but I get the idea she's looking."

"Yeah, right." I tried to spit out the hook. It was a five-hundred-mile round trip for not enough money. "How's the fishing been?"

"As good as it gets. It's making all the guides look like heroes."

"That's not what I hear." Actually, I hadn't heard a thing.

"Goldie," he said. "The cook's name is Goldie."

I gave up. "I guess there's nothing here I can't get out of."

"Have to be tomorrow," Armstrong said.

"Sure," I replied. "I'll be there for dinner."

"There" was the South Fork of the Flathead River and the Bob Marshall Wilderness in northern Montana. It is part of a land the Blackfeet Indians described as the "backbone of the continent," a rugged land of old growth Douglas fir and sheer scarps of mottled argillite that has been carved by glaciers from some of the oldest rock on the face of the planet.

If the four billion year history of the earth—from coalescence to superhighways—was compressed into a single twenty-four-hour day, then the oldest of the rocks we see now in Montana were already here at eight in the morning. The geologic hot tub arrived at about three that afternoon, and Montana began to spend the better part of eternity soaking in a shallow inland sea.

Erosion gullied the high barren plateaus and canyon lands at the edge of the sea. The rivers ran thick with goo, and mountains of mud began piling up at the bottom of the sea. Sometime between eight and nine that evening the first animals, with hard calcium-rich skeletons and shells, appeared in the fossil record.

These animals mixed with the mud and became like coral reefs. The mud and barrier reefs grew deeper and deeper, and so much sediment accumulated that the crust of the earth slowly buckled down beneath the immense weight. Eon followed eon. The sediment was now so thick that the lowest layers of mud and coral had been heated and compressed into mile after mile of solid rock.

With the exception of a volcanic eruption here or an igneous intrusion there, it was a quiet day at the surface beach for Montana until about eleven that night, when the Atlantic Ocean began to open up. The earth's crust was squeezed like cookie dough. The pressure of the spreading ocean left a beautiful land now in the age of dinosaurs all dressed up with nowhere to go. The crust buckled, and wrinkles and folds were pushed into the continental skin of the planet.

About a half hour later—the real time equivalent of one hundred million years—the largest of these wrinkles in the crust squeezed up near the western edge of the American continent. The great layers of mudstones and limestones that had formed at the bottom of the inland sea were pushed higher and higher into the sky. With only moments left in the day that is the history of the planet, this hard rock was finally carved by at least four great scouring ice ages into what we call the Rocky Mountains, and what the wild trout call home.

It is a timeless, enduring land, and it is the land that Hank and Susan had chosen as a symbol of their love some thirty-five years earlier when they were wed in a small chapel in Glacier Park. It was also the land to which they had returned from their home in Texas for a second honeymoon to celebrate their wedding anniversary.

"Hank and Susan are like little kids," said Armstrong, describing the clients I would guide for the week. "Married thirty-five years, and they can't hardly keep their hands off each other."

"Great." I spoke back over my shoulder. I was headed for the kitchen. "A flyfishing honeymoon. We should all be so lucky."

"Where are you going so fast?" he called out.

"I'm just going to see what's for dinner."

"Wait. There's something else I have to tell you."

"What is it?"

"Well. Hell." Armstrong paused long enough to drown a yellow jacket at five paces with a torrent of tobacco juice, then said, "It's about that new cook I was telling you about."

"What about her?"

"There ain't one."

I stopped in my tracks. I'd been had. There was only one thing I could do, and I started with the four-letter pond scum from whence he was sprung.

"Hey," Armstrong's grin was ear to ear, "You leave my mother out of this."

Three days later I was crouched on the shore of Handkerchief Lake, holding the inflatable raft steady as Hank and Susan clambered in for another day of honeymoon fishing. Chickadees trilled as they pecked away at the red rose hips on the verdant bushes along the shore. The sun was just now high enough above the mountains to sparkle on the dark water of the lake, burning off the morning mist, and glowing in Susan's thick auburn hair.

"In that light," said Hank to Susan, "You don't look a bit older'n the day we was married."

"And you," she replied, "You're as handsome as the day you were born."

It was true, but it wasn't much of a compliment. Hank had been born homely. He was so homely he was almost cute, and sported a pair of buckteeth each the size of a buffalo nickel.

Hank pointed to the dimples on the lake. "Will you lookit all them risin' fish," he said in the slow drawl that is peculiar to the south Texas hill country, all the while grinning like a twelve-year-old beaver at Christmas. "Are you ready to go fishin', honey?"

I guess the sight of Hank's smile was too much for Susan, because she leaned over and kissed him, with feeling. They both started giggling. I tried to remember the last time I had heard anyone over the age of twelve giggle. I thought it was probably the rainbow people. All I knew was Hank and Susan had been married about as long as I had been alive, and I envied them for it.

"I'm ready," said Susan when she let go.

"Let's go fishing," they both said together.

It was time to go to work, and I bent to the oars. "Let out about thirty feet of line," I said. "We're over a big weed bed here. If we don't pick up anything on the first pass we'll try it again, and let out more line to get the flies deeper. The best fish will be cruising just above the weeds."

We were fishing a high mountain lake for arctic grayling. Although the surface was speckled with concentric rings left by rising fish, most of the grayling in this lake were feeding on emerging nymphs in the deeper water over the weed beds. Hank was fishing a sinking line, and a soft hackle fly of partridge and peacock. Susan was using a spinning rod and a small gold Mepps spinner, with a soft hackle fly tied on as a dropper about four feet above her lure.

They cast, and in the time it takes to read this sentence they had both hooked fish.

"I got one," Hank cried.

"Oh my, so do I," Susan exclaimed.

It was that way all day long. A cold front was moving down from Canada, breaking down the ridge of high pressure under which we had basked for the past several weeks, and the fish were in a feeding frenzy. Thunderheads built up in late afternoon. Sweatshirts came out to cover sunburned skin. The fish were still biting. A cold wind began pouring down the sides of the mountains, kicking up waterspouts on the lake, and the rain wasn't far behind. Now we would have to hurry.

I struggled into the wind, rowing hard for every inch. It began to drizzle. We were finally back across the lake, nearly to shore, over the weed beds where we had begun fishing that morning, when Susan's rod throbbed, and then doubled over.

"Goodness," she said. The fish took line. "It feels like a big one."

"Hold your rod tip up," Hank yelled, "Remember now, keep it high or the fish will get away."

"Yes, dear." Susan slowly brought the fish to the boat as the cold rain began to fall in earnest.

"Look!" Hank pointed to the end of his wife's line. "There's two of 'em. Big ones."

Susan had grayling on both the spinner and the dropper fly, and they *were* big. The state record grayling in Montana is about three pounds, and had come a few years earlier from this same lake. Together, these twin fish exceeded that record by a good two pounds, and added up to a prodigious chunk of grayling by any standard.

I was surprised; Hank was ecstatic. He could scarcely believe it possible that two fish could be caught at a time, much less that it could happen to someone he had married. Hank (unlike nearly every other husband I had ever guided) was walking on air—and if being truly overjoyed at being outfished by your wife isn't true love, it's at least something like it.

In stark contrast to the revelry of the evening, the following morning dawned dark and dreary. Low heavy clouds you could slice with a dull knife spit rain and sleet. It was midmorning before a caucus of guests gathered near the fireplace, beneath the elk and deer and bear heads. The late start was fine with me, because I was wondering how much wet and cold thirty-five dollars a day would buy.

"Looks like summer is over," someone said, staring out into the gloom.

"That's Montana," said Armstrong, "only has two seasons—winter and July."

"It's just a little rain," said Hank, "Let's go fishin'."

"No it isn't," someone muttered, "It's snow."

"The hummingbirds like it," Susan said, from over by the window where she was watching the feeder filled with sweet red water. We watched as a dozen or more rufous hummingbirds swooped and hovered, the hum of their beating wings audible even over the drone of the rain.

"If anybody wants to fish today," Armstrong brought the meeting to order, "It would be a good time to do some wade fishing. We could hike down Sergeant Creek and fish the Spotted Bear. Walkin' will be a lot warmer than sittin' in a boat all day."

"Well," said Susan, "It will be even warmer in front of this fire, curled up with a book."

"Honey," Hank said, grinning, "If you aren't going fishing, I guess I'll just have to catch enough for both of us."

"I'll be waiting for you," she said, and it wasn't long before I was at the river emptying out the last of the morning coffee. I turned from the tree just in time to see Hank, clad in rubber hip boots without felt soles, swaying alone in midstream. His spindly legs were braced against the current as his feet were slowly pushed downstream over the slippery rocks.

"Hank. No!" I shouted. "Wait for me."

Fifty yards downstream a lodgepole sweeper surged in the rushing water. I envisioned Hank impaled on a jagged limb of the fallen tree. Fishing guides think these thoughts (more often that you might think) because not bringing back fish is one thing, and not bringing back the client another thing altogether.

"Pretty fast," called Hank, edging out another step as I ran to the water still pulling up my waders.

We barely made it over, but it wasn't worth the trouble. The far side of the river was in the cold shadow of a high cliff, and in an hour and a half of fishing, Hank never had a strike. Finally it was time to go back for lunch. The others were already there, and Armstrong had a fire going. We extended stiff fingers toward the flames. "Get anything?" Armstrong asked.

"Nothing," I replied. "Didn't even see a bug, much less a fish. Too cold."

"How'd you do?" asked Hank.

"O.K.," another fishermen replied. "Five over fifteen and some little ones."

"That's great," said Hank.

"That's bad," I thought, even though I knew the guy was lying about the five over fifteen part. I hadn't put my guy on *any* fish.

"All on dry flies." The fisherman was way too nonchalant. "Didn't seem to matter much what kind."

"No kiddin'," said Hank, looking at me out of the corner of his eye.

I spread my arms wide in reply. "We'll get them," I said, "I'm ready when you are."

"Be just a minute," Hank replied. "I'm still buildin' me a bagel."

Hank topped off cream cheese, peanut butter, and black olives with a slice of Walla Walla sweet white onion that was a good half-inch thick. Armstrong pointed at Hank's sandwich, and said, "All that onion you got piled on there, you might be cuttin' your honeymoon short."

Hank grinned, and said there was no chance of that, then we chased lunch upstream with hot coffee from the blue enameled pot, and walked until we came to a small waterfall plunging between two pools.

"That sun sure feels good on my old bones," Hank said. "It's a lot warmer here."

It was warmer. The clouds had begun to lift, and errant sunbeams were now spotlighting patches of orange lichen on the ramparts of steep grey limestone across the river. The feeble rays of the sun were reflecting off the south facing cliffs above the river, concentrating the heat, and warming the water through the long slow pool flowing below.

There was a hatch of mayflies in this warmer water. Olive duns floated in the tension of the surface film, waiting for the weak sun to dry out their wings. It was a long wait, and only a few bugs managed to spread their wings and fly away before they came to the waterfall, where nearly all of the mayflies were being dragged down to the banquet table of swirling currents, and the silver sides of feeding fish glinted deep in the green water.

"Do you see those fish?" I asked Hank, pointing into the plunge pool below the waterfall.

"What fish?" he replied.

"Look for the flashes."

"What flashes?" Hank shook his head in frustration.

"Here, try these." I handed him my polarized sunglasses. "You have to look *into* the water."

He balanced the glasses on his nose, took a good look, then jumped back. "Well, I'll be!" he exclaimed. "What are they?"

"Cutthroat trout, and probably some whitefish."

Hank grinned as he peered down into the water at all the fish. "What fly should I use?"

"Not fly," I said, "flies."

I tied a new leader for Hank, only about seven feet long, with eighteen inches of tippet and a Prince nymph. I then used a clinch knot to tie another eighteen inches of tippet to the bend in the hook of the Prince nymph, and tied in a bright Royal Coachman at the tail.

"Maybe history will repeat itself," I said.

"It worked yesterday," replied Hank, grinning still wider as he thought of his wife and her fish.

Hank began false casting. I hid behind a tree until he calmed down.

Hank was too excited by half, and his thrashing rod reminded me of the beating wings of the hummingbirds we had watched that morning. The scientists say hummingbirds are unlikely flying objects due to their relatively large bodies and small wings, but I was beginning to wonder if they were any more of an unlikely flying object than Hank, if he could just get that rod going a little bit faster.

"Maybe if he had two rods," I thought.

Hank finally let fly with the twenty feet of line he had managed to get airborne.

"Nice cast," I said. "Now just let it swing down through the waterfall."

Things were looking good. Traditional wet fly patterns match the hatch when drowned duns are present. The fish were active, deep, and preoccupied with feeding, so they would not be easily spooked. The plunging current would straighten the short leader, and some of the fish would probably even set the hook themselves on the take.

It did not hurt that we were fishing for cutthroat trout, a fish known for its susceptibility to being taken on the fly, and a breed often disparaged by the elite of the fly fishing community as slightly addled, as small and unwilling to mix it up in a good tussle. Balderdash, I say.

Cutthroat are Montana's native trout, and they have seen it all in the 600,000 years that have passed since they first swam up the rivers. First, they were subject to the ravages of prehistoric predators like the six-foot-long sabre-toothed salmon. Then, the huge volcano that is Yellowstone Park erupted once again, filling the rivers with ash and blocking out the sun. Then the cutthroat had to make it through the Ice Ages, migrating up and down the rivers, coexisting with the hard blue ice that had once been almost 6,000 feet thick where we were now standing. Cutthroat trout somehow found bugs to eat and places to hide, persevering where species perished in the rapidly changing climatic conditions, and they deserve nothing but our respect.

"Besides," I thought from a guide's point of view, "what's wrong with a trout that's easy to catch for a change?"

Hank caught a fish or three right off the bat, and soon his fishing rhythm had slowed of its own accord. I watched a hairy woodpecker tear into a rotten snag for flying ants. A red-tailed hawk soared high above the cliff. Bank swallows began to dip for the emerging mayflies. The trees dripped melting snow as the August sun followed behind the early storm. I was laying in the sun, steaming inside my waders with my eyes at half-mast, daydreaming, drying from the inside out, when I saw Hank hopping madly up and down from one foot to the other.

"Hank sure looks excited," I thought. "That's nice. Maybe he saw a bear."

"Too-too-too," Hank yelled.

I was jolted from my reverie. "What is it?" I ran over. "Did you get stung?"

Hank was still doing a war dance without the feathers, but his grin was huge. Whatever it was, it couldn't be too serious.

"Calm down," I said, "I can't understand you."

He held up his line. Now I understood. Two. Hank had caught a cutthroat and a whitefish at the same time—one on each fly. "Two-two-two," he yelled again.

"I can't wait to tell Susan," he said time and again once he had calmed down, "They won't believe this back home."

We regrouped soon after that, packed our things, and we all

headed up the trail back to the van. Hank and I lagged behind the rest of the group, taking our time on the steep hill, resting when Hank's breath grew so short he could not carry on a conversation. I was a backpacking guide for years, and normal conversation is the barometer I have always used for keeping old hearts in one piece.

Hank was in great shape. He didn't have any trouble at all with the slope. We were up the hill and into the flats, only a few hundred yards shy of the van, and Hank was telling me about the day he was married. "It was just after the war," he said, "Susan was so . . ." Then he stopped, and gave me a quick, puzzled look.

"Oh, boy," he said. He sat down, and leaned against a rock.

"Hank," I said, bending down over him, "What's wrong? What's wrong!"

He stared out at me, then his eyeballs spilled backwards in their sockets. He quit breathing. His head lolled to the side, and with only the bloodshot whites of his eyes showing, his body slumped down.

"Oh, shit," I thought, "what now?"

Cardiopulmonary resuscitation, I remembered, all those years of Red Cross training suddenly of some use. I stretched Hank out on the ground. I tilted back his head, and blew into his mouth, tasting the Walla Walla sweets, watching for the telltale rise of his chest. I felt warm moist air on my cheek, but his chest didn't rise.

What's wrong, what's wrong? The nose, that's it, pinch off the nose, which I did, and began breathing for Hank. I gave him three quick breaths, and then the pupils of his eyes rolled around right side out. He blinked, and stared back out at me.

"I did it," I thought, "It worked. He's alive!"

"Oh, boy." Hank said it again. He took a raspy, bubbling breath; then another. Four more breaths, six altogether, no more, and his eyes spun backwards, buried again in their sockets.

"HELP!" I screamed, "HELP!"

The screams died away. The forest had never been so quiet. I bent back down over Hank, puffing air past his buck teeth into his lungs, then pressing his chest to compress his heart, squeezing oxygenated blood to body and brain.

They never tell you, at those Red Cross classes, how physically difficult it is to perform CPR for an extended period of time. I had only just begun and Hank's shirt was already wet with the salt sweat burning my eyes and trickling down my nose.

They do tell you, at those Red Cross classes, about the Good Samaritan Law. This law says, among other things, that once you begin CPR, you shouldn't stop without a good reason; because if you do, then somewhere, a lawyer in a high-rise office building just might make your life miserable.

I figured my life was already miserable enough without some lawyer messing with it, so it was with considerable relief that I looked up and saw Armstrong and the others. They had finally heard my shouts for help; we set up teams, two people working over Hank at a time, alternating chest compressions with mouth-to-mouth resuscitation, counting the regular cadence in loud voices that still seemed puny and futile against the trees.

"What happened?" Armstrong said.

"I don't know," I said. "He just folded up. He went down like he'd been shot."

"There's a radio in the van." Armstrong started to run down the trail. "I'll go call the ranger station, and see if we can get some help up here."

The ranger on duty in turn relayed the message to the Kalispell Hospital, and a medical emergency response team was sent out via helicopter. Armstrong hauled back a chainsaw, and we felled enough trees to clear a spot for the chopper to land. The rumble of the chainsaw died away. There was nothing to do but CPR and wait.

Hank was now the color of a rotten plum, and it felt as if someone had slipped a sack of quick drying cement into his chest cavity. His lungs would take only a small puff of air, and pressing his chest was like trying to squeeze juice from granite. Then the throb of helicopter rotors filled the canyon. I looked at my watch.

"No way," I thought, but the Timex was still ticking. The chopper dropped down into the clearing. It's an amazing world we live in: it had only been seventy-three minutes since Hank had released his double, and already the nurse was running down the trail, a green box of medical equipment in each hand.

Even now, I can still close my eyes and see her sprinting down that trail.

She was Florence Nightingale to the rescue, her long brunette hair trailing behind, her swinging arms stretching the blue cotton of her uniform tight across her chest with every stride. Her brown eyes peered out through a sea of freckles, sizing up the situation in one quick glance.

"You're doing fine," she said, "Just keep the CPR going."

She grabbed a pair of scissors that could double as hedge trimmers, and sliced off Hank's jacket and shirt. Four rubber suction cups containing electrical probes leading to a chart recorder were attached to his bare chest. Oxygen tubes were inserted into his throat, and we no longer had to breathe for Hank. Drip tubes were set up, and chemicals administered intravenously.

Wow! There we were, seventy-five miles from the nearest paved road, and Hank was receiving the latest in medical attention. Everything was going to work out. I tasted the elixir of hope as I watched the bright green line on the heart monitor jump with every chest compression. It had only been a bit over an hour after all.

"Hank is going to make it," I thought. "This is great. Susan will be so happy."

"All right," said the nurse. "We've done everything we can. You can stop now."

"Stop?" I said, "We can't stop yet. His wife is waiting for him."

The nurse gave me a look of concern. "Look at this," she said, and pointed at Hank's purple face and swollen chest cavity. "He had an aneurism — the major artery to his brain burst, and his blood drained into his chest. He would have died almost immediately."

"But what about Susan?" I said. People don't just die like that. "Hank can't be dead."

"It was only a question of time." The nurse took my hand. "This could just as easily have happened at the breakfast table."

I grabbed a deep breath. "I can still taste the onions."

She shook my arm. Hard. "Are you all right?" she asked.

"He was on his second honeymoon," I choked on the last word.

"He went quickly. There would not have been any pain."

"He was a good guy." I turned away to hide my tears, and leaned up against a tree. "He was in love."

"It's not your fault." She pulled my head to her shoulder. "There was nothing more you could have done."

"He was happy." I closed my eyes. "He had a good day of fishing."

"Maybe," she replied, softly, holding me close, "That is enough."

ABOUT THE AUTHOR

DAVE AMES spends much of his time in pursuit of trout and grayling. He is the author of *A Good Life Wasted: or Twenty Years as a Fishing Guide* (The Lyons Press, 2003), and he has written for the *Chicago Tribune*, the *Cleveland Plain Dealer*, *Sports Afield*, *Fin and Feather*, and *Montana* magazine. He lives in Helena, Montana.

ALSO BY DAVE AMES, AVAILABLE FROM THE LYONS PRESS

A GOOD LIFE WASTED: OR TWENTY YEARS AS A FISHING GUIDE

ISBN 1-58574-631-2

A UNIQUE perspective on an implausible period in the recent history of human civilization. When Dave Ames started guiding, Rocky Mountain locals rode horses and dug camas roots; now they're trading stock options on cell phones. The collision of stone and computer ages was short-lived, but the deep-rooted themes of A GOOD LIFE WASTED remain. A chronicle and celebration of the fishing-guide life, A GOOD LIFE WASTED is poignant and spiritual; it's Blackfoot Indians and copper miners' daughters; it's fiddles and guitars and the fabric of space; it's about what happens to wild people when the wilderness is gone.

"A GOOD LIFE WASTED is a vicarious pleasure for anyone who has ever wondered, even once, what it would be like not to have a 'real job.'"

—*MISSOULIAN*

"[Ames] writes eleven loosely connected stories, eloquently using the medium of angling to discuss the virtues of a lifestyle old timers used to describe as 'trifling.' Moving, thought-provoking, sometimes powerful, and always entertaining, this is an important and welcome addition to the literary side of the angler's world."

—*LIBRARY JOURNAL*

AVAILABLE AT YOUR LOCAL BOOKSTORE OR DIRECT FROM THE LYONS PRESS.
800-243-0495
WWW.GLOBEPEQUOT.COM